Sixty and Speaking Up

An Anthology of Essays Written by
Women in their Sixties Sharing their
Truths, Triumphs and Transitions

Georgina O'Hara Callan

Print ISBN 979-8-9989714-0-2

Ebook ISBN 979-8-9989714-1-9

Contents

To my sons.
Thank you—for your strength, your kindness, and your
unwavering presence through every season of this life
we've shared.

Introduction

Time waits for no woman

This is a book about how women in their sixties, who are undergoing significant life changes, manage the passage of time. Slowly or abruptly, time, which may have been elusive or denied in the past, becomes more plentiful. And within this new space in our lives, and with a new relationship to time, we have the opportunity to look back on our past, reconciling our achievements and successes with our struggles and challenges, while simultaneously anticipating our future.

This is a rare moment in our lives. Because in our sixties we are no longer young but not quite old, we can embrace the pivot point, turning in both directions, backwards and forwards as we shape our identities for the future. Our sixties are a decade in which we come to terms with the past and make plans for the future, and we should use this time well—certainly before we embark on our seventies. To do anything less is a disservice to ourselves.

Almost all women have wondered how, after years of productivity and many accomplishments, whether in a career or caring for a family (or both), we can rationalize the amount of time we have on our hands in the sixties. But this decade offers us moments of grace to rediscover self-worth that may have been diluted over the decades and to reassess and reaffirm our relationships. For some women, time may sit heavily, as days that were once filled to the brim or even overflowing are now empty. For others, the amount of time available during this decade is welcomed as an opportunity to view the world through a different lens, and with a newfound sense of liberty.

Time is a perspective. It is also a gift—one that many of us feel we squander. We assume, sometimes when it's too late, that we have all the time in the world, or perhaps we're comfortable with the idea of squandering time. It's our time to waste, after all, and we're simply executing our prerogative in life to use time as we see fit. When someone complains of being bored, we must assume that they are comfortable with allowing time to pass; it's not anyone else's responsibility to alleviate their boredom or mitigate their state of mind.

With a different view of the world than the one they had in our fifties, many women in their sixties are pausing for self-reflection. The theme of identity is addressed throughout this book as women write about the idea of self. Given that most women care about how they look, all the while acknowledging that how we think we look is connected to how we feel, women have a lot to say about the physical toll of aging, and how the manifestations of age, reverberating around the body, contribute to the idea of a sense of self, of self-worth and self-esteem, as well as a loss of self.

The most significant relationship we will experience in life is the relationship we will have with ourselves. For many, that relationship resembles a romance: an exterior courtship in how we dress and feel about ourselves, and an inner monologue (which changes over time) that deals with the terms of our relationship to ourselves, managing self-doubts, recriminations, justifications, and approval.

The romantic versions of ourselves have to deal with "us" just as we would have to deal with another person, managing arguments, friction, and tension, and, the best part of all, experiencing pleasure and joy—with others, but for ourselves. Joy is experienced alone, because everyone's experience of the emotion is different. Somewhere, we need to find places for all these feelings to settle inside us, like our organs, shifting around to make space for each other over the years. And, as with any relationship, over time, our relationship with ourself changes and evolves, so we become different versions, different iterations of the person we know best.

Moving through the decades from initial independence in our teens or twenties, whether achieved like a quiet transfer of power or a defiant stake in the ground, we become different people over each subsequent decade while somehow remaining familiar to ourselves. It is remarkable when you think about it, given the unforeseen events that occur in each decade, and the circumstances and challenges that can threaten to derail us entirely, that we remain familiar to ourselves.

We don't know with whom we will partner up, if anyone, or how many partners we will have, whether we will have children or not, what will happen to our parents, and significantly what will happen to our lives and when. We cannot predict who will live and who will die, who will sicken but survive, and how life events will shape us. There are changes and adjustments to families and friendships, careers and jobs, and unexpected alterations to where we live and how, encompassing landscapes, countries, and even continents.

No one reaches their sixties unscathed. Encounters with illness, emotional distress, loss, grief, or disappointment take a toll on us, leaving visible and invisible scars. If it's not our bodies that let us down, it could be our minds. People may disappoint us, and relationships may not survive a planned course. There are breakups and divorces, broken hearts and fractured minds in all families, however the word family is defined. Even successful marriages expand, contract, and run over rocky ground. Perhaps a working life or career didn't turn out to be as rewarding as we had hoped. But, over the years, we accept and rationalize disappointments and try to find balance in the pleasures we have experienced.

Here we are, then, in our sixties, each of us with a lifetime of events to review, inhabiting a different body perhaps and a different concept of self. It is up to each one of us to shape our future. We don't have to write ourselves off, or be part of the tropes, the cliches, and the stereotypes of older women—unless we want to; unless we choose to live in someone else's frame of reference. We have the skills, the knowledge, and the capacity to own a version of ourselves that we can craft using the building blocks of our lives. We may identify new attitudes and fresh ways to approach the remaining years in our life, reminding ourselves, daily, that we possess grace, wisdom, and the courage to be the best version of ourselves yet.

I am grateful to the women who contributed to this book. I am thankful to you who are reading this book. I hope that you selected it in anticipation of learning more about other women transitioning through the same decade, that you will find the content insightful, uplifting, and inspirational, and that within the words you will discover encouragement to lead your best life yet, in your sixties.

Those who have shared their stories have written for the women of today and for women of future generations. The baton that was passed from our grandmothers to our mothers and to us has changed, just as we get to shape the baton that we will pass on. How we experience our sixties, and how we approach our seventies, will reverberate over the decades to our daughters, stepdaughters, sisters, nieces, cousins, granddaughters and, eventually great-granddaughters. We are all influencers.

Thank you.

During self-reflection memories wash over you—sometimes a trickle and at other times a flood—along with stories—those you didn't tell your friends and family, and those you barely admitted to yourself—until everything appears before you, unwelcome, and upended like a box of old letters you wish you'd never written.

Chapter One

Women writing for women

This is a book written by women in their sixties for women in their sixties. In sharing their personal stories and amplifying the narrative of being in their sixties, these women are encouraging others who have yet to recognize or articulate their feelings to reflect, to speak up, and to speak out.

In sharing the tales of our lives, we connect through experience. Narratives provide context: where we've been and how we got there. When we share our stories, we're reaching out for recognition, affirmation, and understanding. We hope our words resonate and act as connective tissue, providing points of enlightenment, commiseration, and inspiration. In reading about the lives of others, we have the opportunity to reassess our own lives. Learning about others through their stories helps us explain and understand ourselves. If other people's lives weren't interesting, biographies and gossip would not exist.

The women who contributed to this book bear little resemblance to their mothers. Today, the potential exists to lead longer and healthier lives, although, some would argue that while modern medicine may promote longevity, it does not improve quality of life. Our sixties, nonetheless, are still viewed as the decade of early seniority, and it's the first decade during which we may visit a doctor specializing in geriatric medicine.

For many of us our mothers were perpetually forty-five-years-old—never fifty, and certainly never sixty. But unlike our mother's generation, our birthdays are no longer a secret; there are reminders, in the form of coupons, special rates, and discounts that drop weekly—sometimes daily—into our mailboxes. Our birth dates are on file in many places; we cannot hide.

Women in the past rarely discussed aging, except to pass judgment on the looks of other women. Unless the complaint was about the aches and pains associated with aging, talking about getting old was taboo. Our mothers may have shared their disappointment in how their looks had changed, but they didn't talk about the disappointment inherent in how their emotions had changed, and how they felt. Self-reflection was not encouraged and sometimes viewed as a self-indulgent weakness.

Today, emotional support resources are available as women transition through their sixties. In a world where it is increasingly okay to say, "I am not okay," women can find others to share perspectives and provide guidance; even if this is from social media, podcasts, and online groups, it's far more help than our mothers could have ever imagined receiving.

But for those who frame their views of aging with their mother's perspective, when if sixty was seen as sad, seventy was seen as an unfortunate affliction, women may experience an oppression that weighs heavily with every birthday, like weights being stacked one on top of the other. Do we feel that on our seventieth birthday, the accumulated weights of the previous decades will all come crashing down? And is this a result of not devoting time to self-reflection and preparation, leaving us with a sinking feeling that it's all too late?

Society signals to women, by means of eliminating many from the workforce, that the purpose of their sixties is to transition from productivity to, well, something that looks a lot like less productivity. With childcare, career, and caretaking largely in the rearview mirror, women are encouraged to move away from viability and toward the idea of being on the fringe. The message is that we should pack up and stow away our knowledge, skills, and expertise, now no longer considered useful, and amuse ourselves with simpler, less complex occupations—things older women do in retirement. In short, we are being asked to step aside, and sometimes the invitation does not feel like a request. We are the only people who question what to do with our excess brain power and our acquired skills during this transition. No one else cares.

One of the many themes that women write about in relation to this decade are the practical shifts that take place. Freed from the daily chores of caring, whether that is raising children or looking after older family members, for many women their sixties may be the first time they do not have someone who relies upon them. As liberating as this might sound, it is also frightening. We may have defined ourselves as a caretaker of many people and things in life, and when those responsibilities disappear, who are we now?

Other women have discussed something that reads almost like rejuvenation as they set out to explore new ventures. With their accumulated knowledge, they embark on projects that in previous decades were unimaginable, shocked to find a completely new way to live their lives. One of the many benefits—and there are many—of being in your sixties is that you care less about what other people think. The clock is ticking, and women have rationalized that if society doesn't want our experiences and our skills, we're free to reapply these attributes as, when, and where we choose.

Intrigued about how other women of the same decade felt about being in their sixties, I initiated conversations and discovered that many women were uncomfortable talking about the opportunity for self-reflection, or even how they planned to spend their time. It was as if they were shouldering the attitudes of their mothers. When the topic of their sixties was introduced, women nodded in complicit disappointment of the changes in their bodies and their brains, and looked for commiseration.

There were the expected conversations about health issues and about how the body fails us. The women we once were, decades ago, may be unrecognizable. But no one wanted to talk about their feelings in terms of what they had or had not accomplished, their regrets about the past, and their hopes and fears for the future, or how they had adjusted to life in their sixties.

Undeterred, I wondered if women in their sixties who would not talk would perhaps be willing to write about their experiences. I settled on a title for the book and then invited women I knew to share their thoughts and opinions, asking them if they would like to say something if I provided the framework for them to be heard.

The response was heartening. Friends and acquaintances, male and female, shared the call amongst their friends and acquaintances. If anyone was uncomfortable writing themselves, they knew a woman in her sixties who was eager to put pen to paper. It turned out that there were many women who wanted to have their say, filtered or unfiltered, and these women, like me, wanted to write for other women in same decade.

We didn't want to write about ailments, tricks for dressing for an older body, or makeup hacks. Not one of us wanted to write about dressing with scarves, the age-old safety gift for older women, silently encouraging us to cover up more of ourselves. We didn't want to complain. We wanted to write about our lives in our sixties and the realization of the gift this decade bestows on us, sometimes gently and sometimes roughly, preparing us, if we allow it, for the last decades of our lives.

You will hear many different voices in this book. From snippets of conversations to long-form emails and interviews, I wanted to include the perspectives of women who'd given being in their sixties some serious thought. Some women have chosen to remain anonymous, which is less about the potential for voicing an unpopular opinion than valuing their privacy, being willing to share under a pen name views and thoughts they would never share in public—or even privately with friends and family. For those women who claimed anonymity, a first name pseudonym has been used and any identifying elements of their stories have been changed.

If you would like to know more, there is a list at the back of the book that provides information about the the contributors—the interesting and brave essayists who have written for themselves and for you.

Women have shared, openly, courageously, and thoughtfully, their views on being in their sixties. The stories they relate draw on the sequences and events of their lives and the consequences of their actions that culminate in their views of life in their sixties today. Their narratives are different but recognizable, and I hope that you will find solace, compassion, and inspiration in their words.

Chandra

"In my sixties I discovered tremendous courage to be myself. If I thought I was myself in earlier decades, I was mistaken. Those were just earlier versions of me. Today, in this decade, I'm the best version of myself, and maybe in the future, I'll discover other, even better versions."

Susan

"I wish I felt as good about myself at twenty-eight, thirty-eight, forty-eight or even fifty-eight as I do at the age of sixty-eight."

Maureen

"The events of my sixty-seventh birthday occurred in a predictable sequence. When I woke, my husband had a bouquet of flowers and a card waiting for me on the kitchen table. After forty years of marriage, I'm not surprised—although I pretend to be.

During the day I got a call from my best friend in Florida, a few texts from other friends, and I had a video call with my daughter and grandchildren who live in Michigan. The grandchildren held up pictures they'd made for 'granny' for her birthday. Social media prompted people to send me birthday greetings, with an assortment of emojis, and while it's nice to hear from people, I know they didn't personally remember my birthday. Other birthday wishes came from my ophthalmologist, my insurance agent, the gym, my dentist and other providers that have my birthdate on file. As friends pass or disappear from my life, will this be all that's left—greetings from providers? I guess that's better than nothing."

Chapter Two

Telling tales

When I turned sixty, I felt as if I'd been handed a passport to a new land. I viewed this place as one that was intimidating, not least because our expectations for the transition from the forties to the fifties are quite different than those for the move from our fifties to our sixties. Not for our parents who saw their sixties as old, as a place to age, but for me, active and at least youthful in outlook. What would my sixties hold for me?

Things did not change overnight. The early years of my sixties were not much different to those of my late fifties, and consequently I didn't feel that anything changed or that I needed to adapt. But, of course, lots of things were shifting around me, altering my perception of the world and how the world perceived me, while my body and my mind underwent significant transformation. I was charting new territory with a body and a brain that were different than how they were in the previous decade. I just didn't know it yet.

At the age of sixty-one, I started a new job. Unremarkable, you may think—many women are still working in their sixties, even embarking on new careers—but I'd been self-employed since the age of twenty-seven, and working full-time for someone else was not without challenges. Several of those challenges were age-related. While the environment was multi-generational, more often than not, I was the oldest person in the room.

Five years later, my job ended. Head down over the previous years, immersed in a job that I found interesting and absorbing, I hadn't really given much thought to anything beyond what I was doing at the time. When undertaking the research for this book, I discovered that I wasn't the only woman to live in the moment in her sixties, conveniently blocking out thoughts of the future and omitting to build out any ideas or even make a few plans for my future. Seventy was a birthday I hadn't contemplated, because, somewhere in my mind, the idea of being seventy was inconceivable.

By my mid-sixties, I was in a self-reflective mood. My mind wandered, revisiting decades, surprised by odd thoughts about even odder people, people I glimpsed from my past, popping into my mind without any identifiable prompts. Situations, circumstances, and outcomes came under the microscope, along with uncomfortable feelings about the past. There were also deeply satisfying feelings of gratitude and joy applied to wonderful memories—many better, perhaps, in hindsight.

Delving into one's memory, like flipping through a stack of vinyl records, each cover prompting a memory of someone or something, is the by-product of a planned or unplanned amount of time on one's hands. Driving on the highway one day, a thought that I might be repeating a certain behavior I associated with my mother, a behavior I disapproved of when younger (who am I to disapprove of my mother?), dropped into my lap, and squirmed there uncomfortably. Why was my brain replaying old stories, old wounds, old achievements, and even older events?

Disconcertingly, everything that I'd left unresolved, and unfinished in my fifties presented itself for review in my sixties. All the things I'd postponed thinking about, dreaming about, or even assigning time to regret surfaced at this time, bobbing on the horizon of my dreams.

In comparing myself to other women traversing the same decade, I also realized that I hadn't made plans for how to live the rest of my life. As a two-time cancer survivor, I feel that plans are an elastic concept anyway. The annual pivot point is the routine checkup. While some cancer survivors express an urgency to accelerate the checking of boxes on a bucket list, others hunker down and become mistrustful, living in a narrow world where they feel betrayed by a body they can no longer rely upon. And yet other survivors, like me, take a wait and see approach, open to new things but realistic about how life—and one's body—can strike at you, unexpectedly.

A serious medical diagnosis inevitably prompts questions about mortality, at any age. In your fifties and sixties, as much as you might baulk at the idea of aging, suddenly, getting old seems appealing: "I'll take it, wrinkles and all."

Aging becomes the thing that is desired the most: to get old, and to live for longer. This might leave some people with a feeling akin to intolerance for those who bemoan their age without any context—those who have not confronted the idea that their life might be interrupted early. Survivors may feel within their rights to view this as a violation of life itself, by taking it for granted. The ultimate self-indulgence. When we ask for commiseration over a birthday, are we really saying, "Poor me, I get to turn the page on another year, another decade." Even a flirtation with the concept of mortality should be enough to change one's perspective of the world.

But it often isn't, like a New Year's resolution, it disappears; the promises to find gratitude in everyday, to give thanks, all the good intentions float away, as the wind changes direction and the priorities of everyday life shift about us. But we keep trying.

In previous decades we may have found joy to be peripheral and fleeting, a visitor perhaps, whereas when we're in our sixties, we have the time to devote to identifying and articulating joy on our own terms. Whether a sense of joy is discovered in small corners, or found within an unexpected action, or revealed in a large event involving wholesale change, the idea of finding joy is a worthwhile pursuit as long as the realities of discovery are tailored to expectations. In this book, women write of the pain and joy inherent in a deeper understanding of self, and of how they plan to use their time moving forward by living life on their own terms.

Alice

"There are very few words on a tombstone. If you're waiting for people to appreciate your worth and to recognize your value in their lives, you may find that there's a long wait. Even until death. And then there's no guarantee that you'll be memorialized in a way that reflects your version of you, of the life you led, of the way you want to be remembered.

Claim your value now. You matter now, not later, not in a future that you can't see.

Women who find confrontation challenging often feel underappreciated and marginalized because they hesitate to speak up. But it's up to each of us to stand up and say, 'I matter.' Otherwise, is it anyone's fault but our own if we feel disappointed by life?"

Chapter Three

Deborah Main Jones Latimer

New adventures await

An artisan—a maker of unique, one-of-a-kind pillows—Deborah Main's creativity has defined the past twenty years of her life. Against many odds, having lived with a debilitating chronic disease during the same period, she has built a business of which she is understandably proud. While she approached her early sixties with enthusiasm and optimism, and still feels that way, Deborah's late sixties had a few more unexpected challenges.

"When my mother turned sixty, she called me crying. When I turned sixty, I threw a big party for myself. That, to me, is the most memorable difference between my generation versus my mother's generation. Sixty used to be old. While I understood how my mother felt, at sixty I still looked and felt young.

Going into my sixties, I sensed that there were a lot of new opportunities out there for me. It's odd, but I felt so much more confident entering my sixties than my fifties, as I was passionate about my work and regularly active in the design community.

Even though I hate my wrinkles, the sixties have been an exciting and inspiring time for me. I feel that I've worked hard and earned those wrinkles through years of trial and tribulation as an entrepreneur. Now, in my late sixties, I feel that I don't have to prove myself to anyone any longer, and I have a sense of complete freedom and independence. My sixties feel like a time of rebirth and I find this very refreshing. However, there are many life decisions still ahead that need to be made as I prepare myself for my seventies.

With my children grown up, I no longer feel as needed. I never experienced the feelings that some women have when their children leave home. Once we were empty nesters, my husband and I dove into taking small and big trips together, traveling and living in Italy for three months, really enjoying each other's company, talking about our future together and discussing how we want to age and where we want to live. We were ready and excited to be empty nesters.

While we will always see our children and worry about their futures, they are busy building their own lives. I feel incredibly blessed that I have a loving husband of forty years, and that both our children are safe and happy.

I have recently celebrated twenty years in business, a design studio started purely by accident after I became seriously ill and later was diagnosed with ME/CFS, a severely debilitating chronic disease. It completely changed the direction of my life. I was bedridden for five years, had to quit my job working for a non-profit, and needed to rest for many more years, and still do.

However, creativity found a way to unexpectedly emerge and I started collecting vintage trim and jewelry to sew onto pillows. At the time, I didn't even know how to sew. Since I could no longer work outside of the home, creating pillows became my artistic way of expressing myself, giving me joy and a newfound sense of purpose in my life. It's hard to believe I have made it this far, given the unpredictability of my health, but the life-altering experience of illness helped me find ways to heal and get stronger. Having no design or business background, and struggling with my poor health, I am extremely proud that I persevered for twenty years. I've thrived being part of art and design communities, and I've enjoyed the life-long friendships that I've made while adding beauty to the world, one pillow at a time.

Now, as we begin to downsize our home and our life, confusion and self-doubt have unexpectedly emerged. I thought we would age in place in our home of forty plus years, but traveling to Italy has made me want to create a different life. Plus, I'm finding it harder now to keep up with a home, a yard, and a business.

My energy level and memory aren't what they used to be. I also didn't anticipate that I would lose confidence. I question what I have done in my life, and what I will do now. To be honest, my emotions, goals, and feelings are up and down, and all over the place because I feel as if I'm in the middle of a huge life transition to my seventies, and what that looks like is unknown.

It was maybe when I was around sixty-five, and after recovering from Covid, that I started to slow down with my business and thought, '*What am I going to do with the rest of my life?*' I didn't like the fact that I no longer seemed to have the enthusiasm and drive that I once possessed in my late fifties and early sixties—suddenly, it just seemed to disappear. While I once thought that I would be designing well into my seventies, I feel less interested and more motivated to explore other creative outlets. I still love working with fabric, color, and texture, but it's harder to multi-task and keep track of details. This makes me feel vulnerable, exposed, and less confident. Although this can be scary, I think it's part of the natural aging process, and aging with a chronic disease.

To stay positive during this transition, I try to take things in my stride, to be kind to myself, and remember how much I've accomplished in my life. I feel an urgency to slow down, pause, reflect, and assess what I can and can't do. I want to discover what I really enjoy doing, take better care of my health, and plan for the next decade.

I understand why my husband, David, is hesitant about retiring because he loves teaching and it gives him purpose, as being part of the design community has given me purpose. It's hard to let go of those careers when you are uncertain about what the future looks like.

We've been married for forty-one years, lived in the same house, and we have two major goals this year. To travel to Italy, because it makes us incredibly happy, and we are unencumbered there with the tasks of owning a home and working. This equals a lot less stress which is also better for me. Personally, I want to slow down and create space in my life, have time to sort through thousands of photos and create photo books. The second goal is that now that we've made the decision to sell our home in the next year or two, we need to sort through decades of stuff (including twenty years of business files) and sell my textile, trim, and jewelry collections.

My husband has cared for me, with my disease, these past thirty years but I still worry about how I'll care for him as he ages. I feel that I really need to stick to my most important goal and that's taking care of my health to get more physically fit so I become stronger. I'm hopeful that as we age together, we will be able to create the life and security we desire.

I really want a new adventure for this next big chapter in my life, my seventies. In my mind that would be both of us retiring and maybe moving to Italy for a couple of years or at least living there for three months at a time. In Italy we have less stress and more of a community life. I feel healthier, walk more steps, eat more natural food, and I'm surrounded by art and beauty. I've made some dear friends in Italy. Staying active, meeting new people, and enjoying life-long learning is very important to me. I've started painting and want to learn more about Italian art history.

While there are more life decisions ahead, and less certainty, I want nothing more than to spend the next ten years with my husband, the love of my life, enjoying the simple pleasures of life, family and friends, and traveling together. As I'm near my seventies, and my husband is near his eighties, I feel empowered knowing that every moment of every day counts."

Deborah Main Jones Latimer, Texas, USA

Chapter Four

Lena Samson

Welcome surprises

A deep dive into self-reflection while in her fifties helped Lena liberate herself from her past and successfully navigate her sixties.

"Nothing prepares you for aging. There is no playbook. It can sneak up on you like a thief in the night, ready to snatch your youth away, or smash you like an anvil on the *Road Runner* cartoon.

Turning fifty did not bother me. Still slim and attractive, I celebrated with my first ever trip to Las Vegas with a female friend. I remember how shocked I was by the plethora of happy people, contrasting so starkly with my miserable marriage. I realized that I mattered. My happiness mattered. With half my life ahead of me, maybe, I deserved to be happy so I liberated myself and embarked on my freedom. I retired, traveled, met new friends, enjoyed exotic locales and various boyfriends.

Then, unexpectedly, my first grandchild appeared, and I discovered a new kind of miraculous love, an overwhelming delight in this pure little creature that changed my life forever. Three additional grandchildren later, I'm at peace and blessed to participate in their daily lives. But my journey to this serene state was not easy.

During my fifties I took a deep dive into myself, trying to comprehend the traumas that had invisibly, yet profoundly, impacted my life. It was a time of intense learning, so vital in helping me come to terms with the decisions I'd taken and the paths I'd chosen. Books, professionals, and friends all contributed puzzle pieces to my self-education. Understanding myself led to acceptance, and acceptance led to peace.

I was fortunate that menopause touched me delicately, and not until I was fifty-seven. I'd been active, living my winter dream in a bikini on a Belizean island. Post-menopause my body rebelled, no longer allowing me to lose weight, no matter how strenuously I trained at the gym. I spent the same amount of time on the elliptical machine as always, but one day I saw my heartrate leap off the charts, flashing 'danger.'

Fearing a heart attack, and with fat refusing to budge, I became discouraged and stopped exercising. My digestion slowed to a crawl, too. Luckily, I found a functional doctor who helped guide me through this mystery with the aid of supplements and education.

One morning I found myself repeatedly trying to move a stray hair—or what looked like a spider—out of my left eye. Nothing was there. I became frightened that a blood vessel could have burst and rushed myself to the emergency room. After nine hours and multiple tests, I learned that eye floaters were a 'normal' sign of aging. Who knew? Where was the manual to tell me these things? When my children were born, Dr. Spock's treatise taught me everything I needed to know about childbirth and infancy. Too bad there is no Dr. Spock for aging women.

For instance, now in my sixties, how was I to dress anymore? One day, I found myself standing outside Old Navy and the Gap, hesitant to enter. Was I too old to shop there now? To heck with it, I remember thinking, *I will wear what feels right to me. I'm not about to start wearing a type of saggy house dress, like my mother did.*

However, I did give away five pairs of gorgeous pointy-toed high-heeled shoes that were much-adored during my working life. This donation was easier once I understood that wearing these shoes had wrecked my feet. I loved my shoes dearly, and saw them as symbols of my stylishness, but I hadn't worn them in ten years. Why was I hanging onto them? Like my youth, I bid them farewell, grudgingly accepting that their time in my life had passed.

In another capitulation to age, I surrendered my battle against gray roots and allowed my hair to transform. I wasn't working or dating anymore, so who really cared?

I could always dye my hair again if I felt the need to look younger, but there didn't seem to be any point. This was me now. Me, in my sixties. Yes, I feel invisible and I don't turn heads anymore, but there is a newfound freedom in invisibility. I find that I don't have to beat off unwanted attention, and that's a welcome change.

At sixty-one, I downsized my home and moved outside of town to a peaceful village, across the street from a river. It was the best move I've ever made. I love it here, and I no longer need the possessions and space I once treasured, no longer feel the need to impress anyone. I live on my own terms, not bending my wishes for anyone. I continue to learn so much in my sixties about what is truly important. This is a time of introspection and inner growth, blended with self-forgiveness and a dash of wisdom. I am now on the cusp of sixty-five, and discovering that writing is my passion.

While I expected retirement to be all about travel, my grandchildren have gifted me with all the fulfillment I need. They are my legacy, the most important pieces of myself that will be left behind on this earth. I never imagined that my life in my sixties would turn out this way. What a lovely surprise."

Lena Samson, Ottawa, Canada

Chapter Five

Lesley McKenna

Fending off seventy

Instead of being viewed as invisible, Lesley wishes that older women could have more value in the world. She refuses to be told how to look, how to dress, or how to behave. After a career as a nurse and midwife, and looking after everyone else, Lesley qualified to become an educator, caring for her students as she once cared for her patients. She continues to find creative expression in her work while fending off fears of turning seventy.

"In 2017 I began the decade of my sixties. I didn't know what to expect, except that I'd worked as a nurse in geriatric units, and I'd seen what could happen in old age, how the body and mind could become so frail. This was a terrifying prospect. Now, suddenly, it was here.

My mother hated getting older, and her own declining health—chronic lung disease and advancing dementia—made all that experience personal. So here I was at sixty, acutely and painfully aware of my own mortality, something that has not shifted.

I've found my sixties to be the hardest decade to live through so far. I have a history of mental ill health: suicidal postpartum depression after my son's birth in 1985. Living through an abusive marriage, then divorce, and caring for parents with dementia, which my father also developed after my mother's death, all while holding down a demanding full-time career, was a huge challenge. I was an only child with all the responsibilities; there was no one else to help me.

That all took its toll. In 2019, when I was sixty-two, I had yet another breakdown because of work pressures. Depression and anxiety overcame me, and I took three months off work. As someone who cared deeply about my students and my job, this was a real blow, but it was something of a turning point.

After a lifetime of caring too much about everything, I finally understood that I had to look after me to be able to look after others. It had only taken me sixty-two years to realize this and, like many women of my generation, I had been in service to others all my life—daughter, nurse, midwife, mother, academic, carer—but never to myself.

Accepting that I could care for me was a revelation. I'm now able to say 'no' if I don't want to do something, or if I am unable to do it. Caring less about how other people perceive me has been helpful for my mental health.

I was sixty-three when Covid put us all into lockdown. Despite living with a loving and supportive partner, I felt more isolated than ever before in my life. My friendship circle scattered because we all lived a long way from each other. That circle has never rejoined, and consequently I still feel isolated. Making friends in your sixties is much harder than when you are younger. I'm making huge efforts to rebuild a social life, having joined a quiz group, and I'm attending and running poetry and creative writing workshops.

I try to keep fit by walking regularly, up to twelve miles on occasion, but I cannot exercise the way I used to because I suffer from both hernia and arthritis.

Until recently I was a senior lecturer in creative writing at a UK university. I am now sixty-eight and a writer. I have two adult children, both of whom live someway away from me, and a grandson and a granddaughter on the way.

But I'm staring at seventy in the face, which I hadn't imagined, and my experience has taught me that seventy means 'old.' But I don't feel old. In my head, I still think of myself as thirty. The reality of turning seventy soon is a blow; because of my past experiences in healthcare, the words 'senior, elderly' and, especially, 'geriatric,' have negative connotations to me.

I wish we older women could be seen as something else. Something more. Something valuable, instead of becoming invisible in a society that increasingly worships youth and productivity, as though women in our sixties are incapable of contributing to society any longer. It's as though our experience doesn't matter anymore.

Social media and opinion forums in UK newspapers seem to encourage this attitude, and I've recently noticed a strong dislike of Boomers being expressed by younger generations. It hurts that people like me, who have contributed to society since their late teens, in my case first working in healthcare and, later, in education, are so apparently hated.

While I know that social media is not the real world, I'm aware of being sucked into the hatred it seems to encourage. I've removed myself from most platforms now and I'm happier because of it. I will not expose myself to hatred and I don't understand why others seem to thrive on it. Older women are especially targeted. We're told not to wear bright colors, or colorful makeup. We're definitely not supposed to look sexy. If we try, we are 'mutton dressed as lamb.' Societally, we are presented as being 'past it.'

As I age, I'm aware of every new wrinkle, although I'm lucky that I look quite a lot younger than I am. My body, which I've never liked, has developed arthritis, diabetes, and umbilical hernia. My partner and I no longer have sex. It's harder to keep the weight off, and although I'm not fat, I feel saggy and loose. I feel unattractive, but I will not be told how I should look or what I should wear, or how

I should be. I'm angry at the Western world, which wants to cast us off.

I try not to feel afraid of physical and mental decline, but I am. I want to talk about it with my family, and my partner, but I have given up trying. Much as they love me, they do not want to discuss it, and I just get platitudes back, instead of being able to have a frank discussion. Perhaps they are frightened of acknowledging the future because of what it ultimately means for them.

Taking redundancy in 2024 was honestly the best decision I've ever made. I have a sense of freedom that I've never felt before, and knowing that I do not have to look for another job is liberating. My partner and I have enough to live comfortably, and I'm privileged to own the house we live in. I now have time to write and I'm working on a novel that explores a dystopian world where the insistence on youth and beauty and celebrity worship has taken its toll on a media-controlled society that kills people off at forty-five. I'm starting to approach agents and publishers with another novel; this is something that I didn't have time for before now.

All the while the clock is ticking. But I have to try, don't I? I have to live for now, because after all, what is the alternative?"

Lesley McKenna, Bedfordshire, UK

Penny

"I really didn't think too much about being in my sixties—probably because I still looked to be in my fifties and didn't 'feel' as though I was in my sixties—until the company I worked for was sold, and I found myself without a job. Trying to find a job at sixty-six was a challenge because I couldn't find a job that paid me as much as my previous job, and no one seemed to want my skill set—however many different resumes I wrote or recruitment agencies I contacted.

It all seemed so unfair. I felt discarded. In time, I reconfigured my life, thought about what I wanted to do and what I could do, rather than how much money I could earn. I rescaled my life and today, as a result, I feel so much better about everything."

Chapter Six

A sense of self

Outside the terminal the airport bus waiting to ferry people to another building was already full. Packed with passengers eager to make their next flight connection, each one of us—me included—was carrying at least one bag, a hard-shell carry-on taking up valuable floor space and sometimes a bulky shoulder bag that bumped into the backs of the other passengers. By the time I boarded the bus, there was almost no room to move.

I squeezed into a space standing close to the front of the bus. After a silent negotiation with a row of seated passengers as to where they would position their feet and where I might put my feet and my carry-on bag, I grasped an overhead strap with one hand, and with the other I firmly gripped the long, extended handle of my carry-on bag. From my point of view, I looked like anyone else on the bus. A traveler who was trying to get from one airline gate to another.

As the driver took his seat and started the engine, and the doors hissed closed, I moved my feet slightly apart, anticipating the swaying motion of the vehicle once it began to move. Just as the bus lurched forward, a young woman stood up from the seat next to the front door, put both hands around a metal pole to steady herself, and indicated with her head that I should take her seat. She smiled. I saw that the seat was labelled for the "elderly" or "disabled". At sixty-six I had no visible infirmities and didn't in any way consider myself "elderly". I remember feeling shocked and in not a very friendly way, I shook my head and declined. I didn't smile. I wanted to say, "I'm not elderly. How could you think that?"

Most Western cultures define the elderly as someone who has reached the age of sixty-five. The young woman on the bus clearly thought I was elderly. But before she thought of me as elderly, she must have *seen* me as elderly, as old, and registered that thought before she acted and offered me her seat.

I related this story to a friend, also in her sixties, someone I could rely on to be supportive of me. She suggested that perhaps the young woman didn't know any older people, or didn't have elderly relatives, so to her everyone beyond a certain age looked "old." That may or may not be true, but many women in their sixties do not feel "old" or "elderly," and many do not feel they look it.

"Well, at least you were *visible*," joked another friend. "At least she *saw* you. Older women complain about not being seen—but you were!"

I resolved the matter in my mind by deciding that I must have been tired after a long journey and didn't look like my usual self.

It's true that we rarely ever see ourselves the way that other people see us. We have visions of ourselves that rarely align with the perspective of other people. We see ourselves one way; other people's perspectives are different. It's part of what makes us human—the constant discovery and rediscovery of self. If you've ever walked past a mirror, caught sight of yourself, and thought, *"Wait, that's me?"* you will understand this sentiment.

We have versions of ourselves over the decades, iterations of ourselves in our thirties, forties, and fifties but these versions are unsustainable over the decades, and may have, by the time we're in our sixties, reached an expiration date. Whatever idea of self we have configured by the time we reach our sixties, we must introduce ourselves to yet another version.

In our sixties, we might think that we should have accumulated a resiliency to life, but this is not always the case as new challenges await us. In the absence of a vision for the future, there is an inclination to live in the past, in the days of who we were, and particularly when we were at our most accomplished. There is comfort in reminiscing, but reminiscence works best when it is shared with people who have mutual interest in past perspectives, and over time those people become scarce.

In earlier decades we may have seen ourselves as more athletic, more attractive, more engaged, more focused, more vibrant—just "more." Even as we were defined by the responsibilities we carried in roles such as parent, caregiver, and breadwinner, we seemed more then than we are now. We may have been a stellar employee during our forties and fifties, a loyal and diligent worker, but no one cares about that when we are sixty-five. We may have broken through glass ceilings—in our own way—and established new pathways that other people, in companies we no longer work for, use on a daily basis. There are countless ways in which we may have contributed, but they have no meaning for anyone today—least of all to us.

If we are in possession of the same body and brain throughout life, are we not intrinsically ourselves and when we reach our sixties are we simply just ourselves but older, and possibly heavier with graying hair and more wrinkles? This doesn't seem to be the case. Women in their sixties report that they do not recognize themselves today, describing the process of reviewing photographs of themselves when much younger as if searching for their identities at different stages of life. Scanning images, they look for the woman they were back then, distant but recognizable versions of the woman they are today.

For many women, earlier decades, prior to their sixties were not filled with accomplishments, only duty, and the years of the sixties are welcomed as a platform from which to launch a new version of self. As with any new identity, regardless of how much is retained of the previous iteration, there is the opportunity to look backwards and forwards simultaneously; if we do anything else, we are trying to revert to the past and not embrace the future.

"Being a woman in her sixties means inhabiting a paradox. I have never been more visible to myself and yet often feel increasingly invisible to the world. There is freedom in this invisibility, a release from expectations that confined earlier decades. I care less about appearances and more about authenticity. I speak more directly, love more openly, and choose more carefully how I spend my days."

Barbara Bernier, Florida, USA

Jean

"Generally speaking, I've enjoyed this decade. There are less responsibilities, not having a business to run with the worries of paying everyone's wages. I have more time to myself. I don't socialize as much as I used to and I can be reclusive, especially since lockdown, which I quite enjoyed and believe had a positive effect on the planet, although I know a lot of people struggled with isolation.

I work for a charity where I teach others the skills I have learned as an artist. A friend cares for two elderly ladies and when she needs a break, I step in. It's the easiest work I have ever done, caring for these two women who are in their late eighties and I enjoy their positive attitudes. They say exactly what they like without worrying about what anyone else thinks. As someone who worries that I may appear negative, although I try to be approachable and supportive, I find their attitudes refreshing and hope to be like them one day."

Chapter Seven

Andrea Van Hoven

Discovering a superpower

After a successful career, Andrea upended her life in order to validate herself before beginning the next phase of her working life in preparing for her seventies.

"At the age of sixty-seven (and a half), I left a job that I'd held for nine years. I was the Director of Events for an organization doing development in higher education. My original plan had been to continue working until I turned seventy and then I would begin collecting Social Security. But at the end of the summer of 2024, after enduring yet another reorganization (my fifth) of the team I worked on, I was simply worn out and I felt worn down.

Despite receiving high marks on all my annual reviews, the reorganization process left me feeling disrespected and undervalued. It added to the messages that I was already getting from society that the older you get, the more obsolete and useless you become. It all really got me down. I began doubting myself so I made the decision to resign.

Being the conscientious person that I am (remember all those high marks), I gave the organization six months' notice, which was enough time to get them through the next board meeting, that included a three-hundred-person dinner event. In the end, those six months turned out to be a gift to myself; a time to reflect on what I wanted to do, what I needed to do, and how I wanted to feel about myself and my life going forward.

The first thing I did, mostly out of fear for my financial future, was to think about what kind of job I might want to carry me through to seventy. I knew that I wanted to slow down, work part-time, and maybe have fewer responsibilities, but I still wanted to work, and work for an organization that was engaged in a worthy cause, a cause that spoke to my soul.

I found an administrative assistant position that suited me. There was an initial interview, and then a second interview. Feeling pretty confident about landing the job, I opened an email one day, only to find that the position had been given to someone else. But then came the twist; they wanted to create a new role, just for me, based on my skills with people and events. I was elated. "Ha! Take that," I wanted to yell at my old job—"I do have real value."

But just as quickly, it hit me. I was letting a job and society define my worth. It was a bit of an epiphany. Around this time, I was also doing what so many of us do later in life—reflecting, looking back, and wondering what mark

I'd made on the world. The questions I asked myself were: *Had I made any difference? And if I had, where and how?*

The second part of that six-month gift was time, time to have real conversations with event vendors, campus partners, and others I'd worked with over the years. Part of my self-doubt during this time came from questioning the way I interact with people. I'm not someone who comes on strong or pushes an opinion or agenda. In my period of doubt I'd wondered if that was a weakness in me. But now I see things very differently, and I see my behavior as my superpower.

A pattern began to emerge. I heard the same themes repeated again and again. And those themes echoed even more clearly at my 'goodbye' coffee, where thirty colleagues showed up. In emails and in notes I received afterward, I read the words—grace, professionalism, support, respect, and commitment.

All this has made me excited for what is about to come in my seventies as I continue to work. I know my worth, and it no longer depends on what anyone else says or does. While I know there will be challenges that come with aging physically, I am really looking forward to living my life, for me, and by me."

Andrea Van Hoven, Vermont, USA

Lisa

"I've had two careers in my life, one before my children were born and a second career after my children started to attend school. Now I am retired and I am finding it difficult to fill my days. I was once focused and driven and now I don't know what to do with my time. I feel guilty when I don't have my days scheduled and I'm just shuffling around the house looking for projects. I'm spending far too much time looking at my phone—as if I'll find solutions there! It's difficult to start all the plans I've made for my retirement, it's almost as if I need to grieve first for the 'working' woman I used to be."

Chapter Eight

Peggy Gerber

Thriving as an empty nester

If you had told younger Peggy that one day she would write books, be featured in international publications, and find the courage to be interviewed on podcasts, speak at open mics, and author events, she would never have believed you. Peggy was a stay-at-home mom, raising three children, along with foster kids, and when her youngest child left home, she became an empty nester. She'd reached a turning point in her life.

"While some people find freedom at this empty nester stage of life, I was at a crossroads. I was sixty-one years old. So many of the activities I'd been involved in with my children had ended. I felt as if I'd lost my identity and I was tossed into a downward spiral, developing an anxiety disorder that gradually became so severe that I found it difficult to leave my house. I would lay in bed in the morning feeling as if I were at the bottom of a deep hole with no way out.

Before I could recover and seek help, I reached rock bottom. I sought help with a medical condition I was embarrassed about and I found a therapist, although I was so ill that at first my husband had to take me to the therapist's office. Little by little, I got better. As I became stronger, I poured my heart and soul into healing. As part of my recovery, I needed to find activities to keep busy, so I registered for a writing class at my local senior center, never imagining that writing would be the activity that changed my life.

Words came pouring out of me in torrents as I prepared for each class. Every week I would proudly read my stories and poems to the group, listening closely as they praised my work with lovely comments.

It is no wonder that I was clueless as to how inept my writing was. It was only when I began submitting my work for publication that I realized not everybody loved me as much as my writing class. I received rejection after rejection and I was so discouraged that I almost gave up. But an innate stubbornness kicked in and I turned that despair into determination. Realizing the gaps in my knowledge, I started taking online classes, reading everything I could get my hands on and working hard to develop new skills.

After a while, I began to receive acceptances. One day, I noticed an online contest to write a book and, after staring at the advertisement for what seemed like a hundred times,

I decided to enter. I didn't know at the time if I had what it would take to write a book, but I was undeterred.

I wrote a poetry collection outlining my struggles with anxiety. Although this brought back a lot of painful memories, it became my goal to destigmatize mental health care and normalize seeking help.

As I worked hard to complete my book, my husband was diagnosed with cancer. I felt my world was crumbling to pieces. My husband needed surgery, radiation, and years of treatment. Overnight, I became a caretaker and devoted myself to doing whatever it took to help him through his journey. For brief periods, while trying to quiet my racing thoughts, I worked on my book.

In 2022 I learned that my book had won first prize in the contest and later that year, as I held my book in my hands for the first time, I felt truly grateful that I was able to experience a little bit of magic while living underneath a dark cloud.

While it is always wonderful to win a contest, especially one that you have worked hard at, the best thing about winning was it gave me the confidence to believe that I could write another book. So, I did. My second poetry chapbook was published in 2023.

I have always loved science fiction, finding joy in imagining different worlds, stories of time travel, magic, aliens, and all sorts of weird phantasmagoria, so I hunkered down and went to work. In 2024, my collection of speculative fiction short stories was published. It's a book of magic and imagination, yet I tackle serious issues as well. It will come as no surprise that many of my characters struggle with mental health issues and, although their recovery is sometimes aided by magical potions and mystical rocks, the other recurrent theme is that the characters must always work hard to feel better.

My husband has six more months of treatment before he can be considered in remission. His doctors say the odds are in his favor. We all know that cancer is a beast but whatever happens, we'll get through it together.

My writing career has elevated my status in the eyes of many of my acquaintances; people who would barely nod in greeting before, now want to have a conversation. This has raised my self-esteem. The writing journey I embarked on at sixty-one is an odyssey. I cannot wait to see what happens next."

Peggy Gerber, New Jersey, USA

Chapter Nine

Carol Ascher

No time like the present

A life-long advocate for social justice, Carol went back to school in her late sixties to learn all the things she'd missed the first time around. The oldest by far in every class, Carol isn't in a hurry to earn a master's degree and claims that the marathon journey is far more valuable to her than the sprint to the finish line.

"There are so many life differences in this decade, beginning with retiring from a career as a non-profit executive director and a nonprofit consultant.

This decade has meant finding my way in a world that didn't include professional work or receiving a paycheck, while my husband continued to work full-time. It was an identity shift, giving up a career that I loved but no longer wanted to embark upon, and it took a bit of an ego adjustment to stay in workout clothes all day and not tell anyone what to do, other than myself.

Throughout my adult life, I've been an active volunteer taking on numerous leadership positions. I volunteered for political campaigns, worked as an election day volunteer, and advocated in Washington, DC on behalf of issues that concerned me. I've long been an advocate for juvenile justice, women's rights, human rights, and religious freedom. But in all the years I spent working in the social arena, I never delved into the deep-seated reasons for me to be involved, or to care as much as I did.

In my sixties, I made a huge conscientious effort to learn about racism in our country and to better understand my own personal feelings. I devoted countless hours, something I should have done when younger, to being a better listener and learner on topics of race that were painful for me to hear and to absorb. I became emotionally uncomfortable with what I was learning, and I felt ashamed of my race and culture.

My parents had always preached, 'You can't teach an old dog new tricks' whenever I brought up issues they didn't feel like addressing, but I was determined because of this attitude that I would open myself up, at age sixty-five, to a better understanding in the hopes that I could be more informed by facts and history, and not just by opinion and by rhetoric.

For the first time, while in my sixties, I began to apologize to my children for the state of the environment and the fraught political landscape we would be leaving them. I never felt that way before.

My husband would say my career's crowning glory was in my sixties. At a time when I thought I'd take a big break from my busy life and maybe relax a little, I soon found out that I'm not someone who can lie back and take a break, and I took on a very large volunteer position chairing a multi-million dollar capital campaign, becoming the board of directors' vice chair for an organization that supports boys—around five hundred boys a year—who grow up without fathers.

In my fifties, I climbed a fourteen-thousand-foot mountain and stood on my head in yoga for the first time—both of which were physical goals I set for myself on my fiftieth and fifty-fifth birthdays. In my sixties, rather than setting physical goals, I exercised my mind in a new and different way by going back to school.

A bucket list item that I put off for decades, I decided there was no time like the present to become a lifelong learner. I am now in graduate school and loving every minute of it, maybe because I'm expanding my world of knowledge and critical thinking.

Now I find I spend a ridiculous amount of time studying, researching, reading, and writing, that amounts to probably triple the number of hours that other students spend who are more age appropriate for this challenge. I don't have the technology skills they have, so I devote an inordinate amount of time just figuring out how to perform the small tasks that come naturally to students who are in their twenties and thirties.

I am the oldest by far in every class I have taken, but what I lack in current day knowledge I make up for with the history of my lifetime. Students think differently today than we did in the seventies! Everything is analyzed *ad nauseum* today. I'm accustomed to thinking and speaking in simple terms. Reflecting in depth on topics is not my strong suit, but I'm working on it.

I am in no hurry to graduate with a master's degree. If I never finish, that's ok. It's a marathon, not a sprint, to the finish line and the journey is far more important to me than where I finish.

It makes me so happy to appreciate being in school, something I never did as a twenty-year-old when my parents were paying tuition. My whole life was focused on what came next, how high I could climb, could I break a glass ceiling in the process and what could I accomplish next that was bigger and better than before. Now I'm just soaking up living in the moment and finding absolute joy in my life choices.

When I was in my fifties, both of our children got married and moved back to our hometown. We learned to navigate lives as adults, my husband and I maintaining our roles as parents but with the new dynamic of our children having spouses.

The sixties brought about the joy of watching our kids adjust to having life partners and then becoming parents themselves. I was unprepared for who our kids would become as parents and that has been nothing short of joyous.

The most memorable event during my sixties was becoming a grandmother for the first time at age sixty. We now have five grandchildren, including a set of triplets, and having triplets in the family living just a few miles away has been a revolutionary change in our lives. Living in the moment with triplets has been overwhelming, exhausting, and extremely joyful, sometimes all at the same time.

I want to travel more, workout five or six days a week, try new things and be adventurous. When my parents were in their sixties, they slowed down significantly, but I just want to do as much as possible, figuring I can rest when I am dead. I don't take good health for granted, not for a minute. I'm surrounded by relatives and friends with devastating health issues, but I feel blessed to be healthy and strong, something I work at conscientiously.

Perhaps I fear aging, or maybe it's vanity, or maybe it's because I am an overachiever? Mostly, I think it's because I don't want to give in to the 'old age adage.' At some point, I know I will, but not in my sixties."

Carol Ascher, Louisiana, USA

Trina

"All my life I've admired strong, and sometimes defiant, women. The kind of women who always chose to live life on their own terms, even if those terms made them seem like outsiders to everyone else. Now, in my sixties, divorced, with my children settled in their own lives, it is my chance to be one of those women, unfettered by my own ideas of self—and other people's ideas of me, of who I should be. I can be that woman who does what she says and says what she thinks—and that includes the words 'no'—an independent thinking—and acting—woman."

Chapter Ten

Silvia Smith

Hiding in plain sight

Silvia divides her life into thirds. The first third she devoted to identifying a career, getting married and having children. For the next third Silvia raised children, worked and cared for elderly parents. The last third is dedicated to Silvia making peace with her life and giving herself the break she feels she deserves from the years when she was responsible for everyone else.

"My mother used to say that it did not matter how young you looked; the years are still there. I gaze at my face in the mirror. At sixty-eight years of age, I have no wrinkles. My hair needs to be touched up every three to four weeks as it has gone gray and while I'm a bit curious to see how I would look with a headful of gray hair, I'm not prepared for that yet.

People are very gracious and tell me that I look much younger than I am. I feel flattered, but my body does not agree. My knees hurt, and every morning there is a new ache somewhere in my body. I get tired more easily. While I love looking after my grandchildren, keeping up is becoming harder. They want me to play on the floor with them, which I do, but it is a monumental task to get up. They proffer their hands and giggle as I strain and grunt, rolling onto my knees before finally raising myself to a standing position.

The physical side of getting older is annoying, but I'm lazy about keeping fit. I do enjoy leisurely walks in the nearby woods, where observing the trees gives me pause to reflect and give thanks that I've come thus far.

As a young child, I lived in a home rampant with abuse and chaos. But over the years, I've learned to treat myself with gentle, loving hands and I've never felt more at home in my own skin. When I look in the mirror, I'm proud of the person I see, someone who is good, brave, and resilient, someone who has so much to offer my loved ones. I have healed the child who was hurting inside me for so many years.

In my early thirties, I was diagnosed with bipolar disorder and subsequently lived with a sense of shame and guilt for most of my life. Now, in my late sixties, peace has settled on me like a gentle dusting of snow. I've accepted the fact that bipolar illness played a key role in my erratic behavior before I was accurately diagnosed and treated. Rather than focus my energy on blaming myself, I blame the illness for causing these actions and reactions.

Riding an emotional roller coaster is an apt metaphor for living with bipolar illness. My family witnessed the crashing depressions and hypomanic episodes created by this chemical imbalance. The efficacy of medications wearing off and life stressors contributed to my symptoms. At this point, I have reached a marked stability with regular doctor visits and ongoing therapy.

My husband was a church pastor for thirty-eight years. Though it was rewarding work for him, it was also extremely hard on me. While he looked after a sizeable congregation, I was often left alone to raise our three children. I also tried to hide my illness from church people for fear of stigma. That took a toll on me. I always looked forward to his retirement and the day when we would no longer live in a fishbowl.

My life prior to turning sixty had been taken up caring for my children, and once they were gone, my parents and in-laws needed to be looked after. Losing all our parents was hard, but it meant not having them to worry about during the pandemic.

During the first half of my sixties, I was still busy enjoying a career as a teacher of English as a second language. Teaching in an assortment of venues, I met interesting students from all corners of the world. Preparing relevant and thought-provoking material, and energized by encounters with people every day, provided a nice structure and routine to my days. I felt productive and useful. Then Covid hit and in one fell swoop I lost all my teaching contracts. I stayed home and felt lost at first and, like the rest of the world, hunkered down and wondered how long the pandemic would last.

As my sixties brought a modicum of relief and freedom from responsibility, and as I'd long harbored an ambition to write, I took the opportunity of empty days to finally put pen to paper. I woke up early and in the quiet morning hours began to write poetry. Soon I'd accumulated over a hundred poems and decided that it was time for me to invite the world in to share my thoughts and feelings.

After engaging a local publisher, my book of poetry became a reality. It was an instant success: I sold many copies and received positive feedback. At the age of sixty-four, I'd achieved confidence in myself as well as the courage to publicly share my journey in life and, if it was a mistake, I had the courage to deal with it. Fortunately, the opposite happened. Readers thanked me for raising topics normally hidden from view.

After retiring from teaching, I've never looked back. I learned how to quilt and honed my sewing skills and made tons of items for my grandchildren. I continued to write and published another book of poetry, and I now offer poetry workshops at our local library and writing association.

Last year, I was diagnosed with uterine cancer which, fortunately, was caught early. I pray for good health because at this stage in my life that is a top priority. My husband and I live a quiet life in a small town and see our grandchildren often enough to keep us feeling young. We are thrilled to be an active part of their lives. I take one day at a time, do my best, and give thanks for a wonderful partner to share my days with and that I have finally found my voice in writing."

Silvia Smith, Ontario, Canada

Deanna

"I think of my decade of the sixties as being a time when I can write my own script. This takes courage. But if I write my own script I should also be able to create my own ending to my story and by that I mean, decide the terms of my retirement and old age. I don't want to leave things up to chance. I am deciding now—albeit a little late at sixty-seven—how and where I want to live and to whom I should leave my hard-earned money. No one wants to talk about this, except attorneys, but I don't want to leave things up to chance and I want to plan now. I believe this is one of the purposes of our sixties, to plan for the next few decades."

Chapter Eleven

Barbara Bernier

Reinvention

Retirement was both welcoming and intimidating to Barbara, offering her the previously unthinkable gift of time and simultaneously prompting questions about what to do with that time. During a reinvention of time, and of self, she discovered things that she had longed for, such as a spiritual practice that embraces questioning rather than certainty. At an age when society expects older women to step back from innovation, Barbara is mastering recent technology.

"As I sit here in the quiet of my study, I find myself reflecting on this remarkable journey of being a woman in her sixties. There is a certain clarity that comes with this age, a perspective that I could not have imagined in my younger years. Over the last decade the landscape of my life has shifted dramatically.

Last May, we celebrated my daughter's graduation from college. Our youngest child, now holding her diploma and heading out into the world. As I stood there watching her in her cap and gown, I felt a complex mixture of immense pride and unexpected emptiness. For over thirty years, my life had been structured around raising children, their schedules, their needs, their dreams. And now, that chapter has gently closed and I found myself standing at the edge of a new frontier, asking that perpetual question: *What next?*

Retirement appeared on the horizon like an approaching shore. For more than twenty years, I was a law professor and leader in legal education. With significant administrative experience in establishing nascent law schools, as well as program development and implementation using EQ and contemplative practice techniques, constitutional and property law courses were my primary focus and, more specifically, issues concerning gender and the international rights of women. While teaching a summer course on that subject in Innsbruck, Austria, I was fortunate to co-teach several classes with Justice Ruth Bader Ginsberg—truly an honor and a highlight.

Towards the end of my career, I filed a lawsuit regarding the for-profit law school where I was employed. At that point (having been tenured at two other nonprofit institutions) I thought it was a way to explore the 'disruption' of legal education, only the find that the corporate law school model does not serve its students but its corporate shareholders.

I soon left this institution and filed a whistle blower suit against it. Although I left full-time teaching, I maintain that my decision to do so was based on integrity and honesty.

Having finally stepped away from the daily grind, the morning alarm no longer dictates my days. Time, once my scarcest resource, has suddenly become abundant. It's taken me months to adjust to this new relationship with time—to understand that I can linger over morning coffee without guilt, that my days belong entirely to me now. But guilt creeps in, as old habits take time to change.

This newfound freedom has allowed us to travel in ways we never could before. Last autumn, we spent three weeks in Paris and in Reims, renting a beautiful contemporary apartment right in the middle of the bustle of the Marais and a small apartment among the vineyards in Reims. We explored the region unhurriedly, discovering small family wineries tucked into hillsides, sampling local cuisine, and watching the harvest come in. There was no rush, no countdown to departure, just the luxury of being present. In Spain, we walked portions of the Camino, not as pilgrims with a destination, but as travelers embracing the journey itself.

In spring we ventured to California, not the hurried week-long vacation of our working years, but a slow, meandering journey. We rented an apartment near Muir Beach and lived like locals for a month. I brought flowers at the market, meditated on the beach, and spent afternoons in museums getting lost in the beauty of art. Slow and methodical were we, the quiet and the beauty of our surroundings providing a unique perspective. At a national shoreline park, I discovered that the beauty of watching seals sunning themselves on the rocks was miraculous.

Once of the most profound changes in my life has been taking Jukai in the Buddhist tradition. The ceremony of receiving the precepts connected me to something I'd been seeking for years; a spiritual foundation that embraces questioning rather than certainty. The sangha has become my refuge during these turbulent times, offering a community of fellow seekers who understand that sitting with discomfort is often more valuable than rushing to solutions. In a world that seems increasingly fractured and chaotic, this practice provides me with a center of gravity and a way to engage with difficult realities without being consumed by them.

I have discovered that this phase of my life demands reinvention. Rather than retreating, I've found myself curious about new frontiers. Last year, I began exploring artificial intelligence and its applications, something I knew absolutely nothing about six months ago. Now I'm taking courses, attending workshops, and even exploring freelance opportunities in this field. The digital landscape is constantly evolving, and this is something that I am finding invigorating rather than intimidating.

My children are amused (and occasionally impressed) by my determination to stay current. I'm now working on a course and a manual that will adopt AI methodology around legal relationships that college students and young graduates encounter as they move into their careers. The manual will cover matters such as employment contracts, landlord-tenant relationships, credit, roommates, and other matters of legal importance to this age group.

Health, of course, hovers in the background of all these considerations. I'm fortunate to be well, but I no longer take it for granted. The small aches that arrive with the morning, the occasional forgetfulness, the need for reading glasses, these are gentle reminders of time's passage. Friends have begun to face serious diagnoses. Some have already departed. Mortality has become less of an abstract concept and more of a quiet companion. Rather than dreading this awareness, I find it clarifying. It strips away pretense and focuses attention on what truly matters.

I think often about legacy now, not just in terms of worldly achievements, but in the quality of connections I've fostered, the kindness I've extended, and the wisdom I've hopefully gleaned and shared. There is an urgency to experience fully, to savor deeply, to love generously. Not because time is running out, but because time itself has become more precious.

So here I stand on the threshold of what might be the richest chapter yet. Not young, but not old. Not the beginning, but far from the end. I'm carrying the wisdom of decades lived, yet I'm still curious about what lies ahead. This is the gift of being a woman in her sixties and beyond, the beautiful complexity of looking both ways, backwards with gratitude and forward with hope."

Barbara Bernier, Florida, USA

Chapter Twelve

Eileen Keller

The clock is ticking

Living has a different perspective after receiving a diagnosis that defines the limits of one's life. Eileen feels fortunate to be alive in her sixties, still living, still learning, still loving and celebrating "having it all".

"Someone once asked me to undertake an exercise to determine happiness. In the morning, I was to wake up, but to keep my eyes closed. Then I was to imagine exactly what I needed, and where I needed to be to feel accomplished, safe, happy, and well. As a single mom, I never had time to stay in bed pondering, so I gave it a good two minutes and then got up without a firm answer.

The next day, I tried again. But basketball practice started at sixty-thirty a.m., and I still had not made breakfast or lunch, so the exercise had to wait. Of course, I thought about my lack of all the things I needed to make me 'good' during that day, but for what it's worth, these things did not create a formula to determine happiness.

I decided that I'd complete the exercise the following morning, but once again, my brain forgot to think about happiness. Maybe there was just too much to do?

Fast forward twelve years and the basketball player son graduated from college, started his own company, bought a house, got married, and is now a father, and I have a granddaughter. My early mornings are about wrapping up housework in an hour and enjoying my new Hubba Hubba in our cottage home. I'm married! After almost thirty years of being a single mom, I decided to go all-in, or nothing, with my relationship man. Why? In July of 2024, I was given only five more years to live due to complications from a surgery four years prior. The good news was that the surgery occurred after I turned sixty-five and Medicare was in place to pick up the million-dollar tab. Living to be sixty! What a ride!

My son and his wife are great people, both fully employed so that they can afford their middle-class American existence in 2025. My daughter-in-law had been on paid maternity leave for nine months, but she went back to work recently, part-time, and remotely, and now wants to stay home as a full-time mom. My son says that they cannot afford to live only on his income, so they asked me, and the other grandmother, if we could step in and hold a summer camp for their daughter at their house. Fortunately, our granddaughter is an exceptional eight-month-old delight. Both grandmothers said, 'Yes.'

Now I'm sixty-nine-years-old, still running a business (or two), married, and taking care of a charming eight-month-old granddaughter ten hours a week. With eyes wide open, I realized that this was my first time taking care of a child. After the first hour of summer camp, I told myself that I couldn't do the task. My own children were always in school or in the care of a beloved nanny so that I could work, attend meetings, and put money on the table.

The constant actions and reactions of my beloved first grandchild felt like a strange escape room game, with the ticking of the clock being the only solution. I started thinking, doing the math in my head. My mother was twenty-six when I was born, her mother was seventeen when she had my mother; that means my grandmother was forty-three when I was a baby. Forty-three! And here I am on the floor encouraging my granddaughter to crawl, and I am sixty-nine. This brought me more joy than all the clients in the universe.

Our generation of women can really have it all.

Last year, I was working with a woman who was twenty-six-years-old. She was focused on finding a 'quality-of-life' job. I wanted to tell her that she needed to find a job, or an activity, to fulfill her needs for living in Austin, Texas (money, family, friends, housing etc.), and then focus on her quality of life, once she had the basics in order. But that didn't feel honest. I have been working since I was sixteen years old, and I was just getting my quality of life in order now. Wouldn't she have to wait that long?

I remembered many years ago standing in our suburban kitchen with my family, my husband at the time holding a small child, my daughter, and my step-daughter. My husband's mouth was moving—but I was thinking about all the things that I needed to do. It was Mother's Day, and I was hosting a luncheon for his grandmother and mother, and I still had a to-do list of seemingly 4,000,000 things.

I looked at him and heard him say, 'Since it's Mother's Day, we would like to all do something with you that YOU want. What would you want to do?' After I understood what he'd said to me, and thought about it, I started crying. I had forgotten what I liked to do. I could not remember what brought me grace and joy. Why, then, should a twenty-six-year-old be able to just click her ruby slippers together and immediately get a quality-of-life job, instead of, like me, paying her dues?

For my quality of life, today, I've put together the pieces I need to make it happen. First of all, I need to learn to say 'no' and only do what I want to do. Secondly, we should celebrate anything and everything, early and often (I was born on a Saturday, so now we celebrate my birthday every Saturday). Thirdly, my Hubba Hubba and I met on the nineteenth day of the month, so we celebrate our anniversary every single nineteenth day; we even got married on the nineteenth day of the month so that my husband could remember the date.

Another important piece is creating traditions that don't interfere with the in-laws' celebrations of holidays. For example, organizing eating pie the morning of Thanksgiving for the whole neighborhood instead of a midday meal, celebrating Epiphany instead of Christmas, filling our house with music every morning and evening, and hosting full moon concerts in the backyard. Add to that laughing, dancing, singing, and having play time every day. Lastly, sending someone a handwritten note every day and reminding them how much they mean to me, and standing, every morning, in the front garden with coffee grounds in my cup, and telling the Universe, 'I am here.'"

Eileen Keller, Texas, USA

Pam

"If we're here, just visiting, for eighty years or so—if we're lucky—we should tread lightly, lovingly, and considerately on the planet and treat each other well. What is the point of accumulating power if you choose not to use it well? And money, why hoard it? Just disburse it in your lifetime; you can't take it with you."

Chapter Thirteen

M.J. (Em) Buckman

Defining identity

By the time M.J was in her fifties, she realized that for most of her adult life she had pretended to be someone she was not. Behind the masks she wore was someone who struggled with mental health issues, which eventually resulted in an attempt on her own life. But on her sixtieth birthday, M.J. published an award-winning book based on her life. She now delves back into her experiences to help other women move forward.

"The concept of identity has always fascinated me: my own identity and that of other people.

My first iteration of self was in my teenage years, when I was befriended by a group of exotic and interesting young gay men who encouraged me to become an outgoing, gregarious socialite, immersed in gay culture. This was followed by a period of feeling that I had to be sensible, and my identity was very much bound up with my career and being a dutiful wife and daughter.

Menopause, divorce, re-marriage, caring for elderly parents, my place in the world was defined by the roles I'd acquired—roles that I relied upon in turn to define myself. But the roles began to disappear. My children needed their own space to go their own ways, my career was over, my role as caretaker was finished, and my mental health was suffering.

I've been acutely aware of the changes in my life. I'm someone who analyzes everything that happens to me, everything that is said to me—and I mull endlessly over it—which can be useful to me at times, but it is also self-destructive.

Attempting suicide was the only way to stop the demons in my head who were constantly telling everything that was wrong with me, that no one liked me, that I didn't deserve to be loved or even to live, that everyone would be better off without me. I'd always thought about ending my life— suicidal ideation, it is called—but I never thought I'd act on these thoughts. Until I did.

After a massive overdose, from which I didn't expect to survive, I spent two days in hospital in isolation, re-evaluating my life in a way I'd never done before. I lay in the hospital bed thinking about what I'd done, who I was, and what I was going to do.

Back at home, my antidepressant medication increased, I turned to what really helped me, and that was to write. I began to write about my life and found that I couldn't stop. I wrote blogs on LGBTQ culture and on mental health. I did research for my first book, which was published in 2023, and now I've published my first novel. During this process, I found an online community of writers and readers from all over the world.

Writing grounds me. It gives me the opportunity to express myself, to learn, and to explore. In some ways, it has saved me. In my sixties, it is now often the thing I choose to do above everything else—along with walking in the countryside.

I've learned that it is okay not to be okay, that I don't have to hide behind a mask, and that not everything that happens to me is because I'm a bad person. Writing about it all has been cathartic.

When I realized that other people thought I'd written something of worth, I allowed myself to feel a degree of pride that I'd managed to turn my darkest moments into something positive.

I've also volunteered all my life, and now I'm choosy about what I do and how much I offer—that is an important lesson I've only recently learned. If a situation or person makes me feel uncomfortable or triggers my stress, I walk away.

With the support of my husband, I have also walked away from toxic relationships in my personal life. I've always been a people pleaser, and that is something I am less willing to do these days. It means that I am no longer in touch with a couple of family members and a few friends, and although that hurts, it's the healthier choice for me.

I'm still here, I'm doing something positive with my life, and I have people who love me. That is enough."

M.J. Buckman, UK

Chapter Fourteen

Elise Krentzel

Aging backwards

Like Benjamin Button, Elise believes that you can age back-wards, but first you have to recognize yourself and come to terms with the fallout of past decisions that have placed you where you are today. Only then can you move toward tomorrow.

"At sixty-five I felt more invigorated and freer than ever before. Now, at sixty-eight, I am hopping around and jiving to a new beat, one familiar on a soul level yet foreign in practice.

The fresh rhythm resonates with the boundless opportunities that my teenage self once envisioned, where every closed door unveiled a new window of possibilities. Love thrives in a world where my spirit and the natural world interconnect, from the small to the grand. My world is a place where noise is deflected and sent back to its rightful owners — those who hate, complain, and mandate their fear-imprinted ideologies onto others.

This brave new world of mine is not *la la land*. It is a magnificent flowering garden of ideas and movement. I am free to extend my dreams in any direction.

While turning the corner of sixty, I began taking a particular interest in how my physique was changing. I didn't like the extra flab around the back of my elbows, nor the small, but spreading, bald patches near my forehead. The cauliflower growing on my upper arms was a garden of defiant and unruly craters in its texture, and in some places on my body long stretch marks of needlepoint reigned.

My breasts hung slightly lower than in their perkier, younger days. Each time I clasped a bra closed, I had to nudge my breasts into the cups to keep them in their rightful place. I ditched those bras and got myself ones that did not require any assemblage, but I still had to uplift my friends. I would say that the worst thing I experienced was incontinence.

Yet having accepted the changes, outside and inwardly, now I embrace my body and lovingly adore what I see in the mirror. My face, elfin in nature, is identical to my baby pictures and instantly recognizable. Playing music invites me to bop and prance around my apartment while serving as a workout to get my steps in. Whenever, wherever, with or without a reason, I dance, even in supermarkets.

Without fear, favor, or regret I shed many so-called friends. I'm short on time, low on tolerance for nonsense, and I couldn't care less about others' opinions of me unless

I have inadvertently hurt them. Sometimes, I can be clumsy in my directness! I was told by one of my only remaining childhood friends that at this age it is hard to make friends because everyone is set in their ways. And she is right. My approach now involves thoughtful discernment and moving beyond superficiality, which I find tiresome. To me, the worst offenders are people who gossip. I reject that as childish behavior.

I am aware that I can be overly harsh or politically incorrect with my younger colleagues due to my lack of knowledge about the lingo, but I do not want to compromise. I am a writer, after all. When empty space fills up a room, I do not run or fill it with extraneous drivel like TikTok or Instagram or binge on Netflix.

I changed my eating habits one-hundred-and-eighty degrees because I want to live past one hundred years, like so many Japanese people. I eat red meat only one to three times per month, fish three or four times a week and the other nights I eat vegetarian-based dishes. Once a week I eat chicken.

As part of this dietary revolution, I donated to the local food kitchen every last packaged item, all the canned goods in my pantry with all processed sauces like soy, oyster, dressings, tomato etc. Now I use only VO olive oil, made in Japan, sesame oil, and pure organic avocado oil. I decline dinner invitations unless there are pure ingredients on the menu. I lost twenty pounds not because I wanted to but because eating healthier produces a healthier body.

Most importantly, I forgave all my wasbands, especially the last one, the father of my only child. Self-forgiveness presented a significant challenge but I was obligated to.

I craved love again and realized it would not manifest itself until I freed myself from the past. The kind of love I wanted was not ordinary. I have experienced the physical, emotional, and intellectual aspects of love, each as separate parts of a structure I was building. That structure was me.

First up was self-love, because in my case I knew that in order not to settle with anyone, I was required to find the 'whole package' divinely wrapped in me first. With the next love of my life, I want to share values, not traits. I do not judge myself against others who date often or might obtain new partner(s) before me (btw, I'm still single but receptive).

Now that I have my own house in order on both subtle and sublime planes, I can be the person I always was without the trauma of my past or the emotional baggage from the fallout of past decisions. This is my secret for aging backwards, just like Benjamin Button. And no, you don't have to take any of those expensive supplements that age you backwards. Do it from within."

Elise Krentzel, Texas, USA

Chapter Fifteen

Seeing ourselves

The mirror does not lie

I looked forward to meeting a friend whom I hadn't seen in thirty years. We used to be very close, but the trajectories of our lives, and thousands of miles, had interrupted our friendship. Now, finding ourselves in the same city at the same time, and both in our sixties and curious about each other, we'd agreed to meet for lunch.

Prior to the meeting I'd sent her a text message, pointing out the obvious—"Just so you know, I'll be wearing my sixties face"—in order to preempt a shock she may experience at seeing me in my sixties rather than my thirties. I also wore dark sunglasses so that my eyes wouldn't reveal any reaction to seeing her face, which was once so familiar, now lined and thickened.

At some point in my sixty-ninth year, I realized that my face was settling into the face I would be wearing for the next decade. I'd seen this face on older friends, women in their seventies whose faces had seemed to settle and thicken, or shrink and cave, so I knew what to expect. If there's any doubt about aging, a quick check of an old driver's license tells you everything you need. We looked one way then, and we look a different way now.

Conversations about looks lead inevitably to conversations about makeup, and I discovered that there were two distinct groups of women willing to discuss this topic.

Firstly were women who wore little or no makeup and didn't see any point in making up their faces to present to the world a different perspective of their identity. It's not as if these women didn't care about themselves; it's just that they choose not to be concerned about how the rest of the world views their faces.

The second perspective was from women who'd always worn makeup and paid attention to their faces, spending time and money on preserving their looks and adapting them to each decade. Or perhaps they were attempting to maintain the same look over the years, in chasing a consistent vision of themselves, even as they acknowledged the changes in their faces that signaled the aging process to the world. Many women in this group reported that makeup is part of their identity.

The theme that was most often voiced in discussing makeup was one of using makeup to maintain, as far as possible, a vision of self that referenced an earlier era—an era when makeup was used as a method of attraction and to elicit appreciation from other women, as well as men. This was an era when women were more satisfied with how they looked and how the rest of the world viewed them, reflected in everybody else's eyes.

Carla

"Makeup is my best-friend. I've always loved makeup, since I was a little girl. For me, make up is part of a fantasy, a fantasy of being someone else or at least a part of myself that I show to the world—an extroverted version of me. Makeup not only helps conceal the parts of me I care not to show, but it enhances other features, what I consider to be my better features.

I love makeup counters and new products and makeup tutorials, and all the illusions and changes that makeup provides, and I'll continue to apply make up for as long as I'm able to hold brushes and sponges and apply eye shadow and lipstick without my hands shaking—and even then, I might find someone else to apply makeup for me.

I don't feel the need to justify this to anyone. This is me. I'm entitled to play at dress-up, which for me is also makeup, for as long as I want, and I refuse to be restricted by other people's idea of age. I know that looking good is my own personal definition and not necessarily anyone else's definition; it's part of who I am. That doesn't mean that I'm an unserious person who doesn't care about social issues, or an insincere person: it just means that I like to make myself up."

Annette

"Makeup for me is war paint. I feel I need this paint, this protective layer, not only to shield my more introverted self from the world but to establish my place in a world that can often seem hostile to women. Once I put on makeup, I feel confident in taking my place at the conference table. Even the act of putting on lipstick before leaving the house is a form of ritual preparation to go out to battle."

Joan

"If you are asking me if women who seek out face lifts and surgical corrections are in pursuit of an improved, in their eyes, version of themselves I would have to agree. I think these women are dissatisfied at a fundamental level with their relationships, their lives, and the person they see reflected in their eyes.

While it's not fair to say that everyone who seeks out needles and scalpels is searching for an improved version of themselves—and women will tell you they are doing it for themselves, and not anyone else— there's an underlying theme that if one isn't happy with oneself, and if I looked better/different/more attractive, I'd attract better/different/more attractive people."

May

"Makeup is, for me, a form of nostalgia, back to a time when I loved to dress up and go out and about and explore the world, interact with people, flirt, entertain, and have fun. Makeup reminds me of the good times when I was young and carefree. I put on makeup to go to the grocery store or to the post office and I see this as a not having given up on myself, or on my life."

Kelly

"I'm a vain woman. It's taken me to the age of six-ty-four to admit this, but I'm vain. My mother was vain, obsessed with her appearance, and I put that down to her low self-esteem but the same must hold true for me. On the surface, you might not think I had any issues with my looks, or my confidence, but I do. Particularly in this decade, when women I know are less focused on their looks, I realize that I pay the same amount of attention to how I look as I ever did.

I miss the attention of men looking at me, and when I mentioned this to a group of women friends, they were all shocked: 'Is that how you judge yourself?' they asked. I was embarrassed, but the truth is I still want men to look at me and admire me. I still want to turn heads, although the kind of men who look at me today are not the kind of men I'm interested in, and this just makes me feel depressed.

My vanity causes me to over-think many things. I fret about my hair and makeup and my body and my clothes. Going out somewhere special triggers a lot of anxiety about what to wear. But if you met me, you would have no idea about any of this, or how much time I spend in front of the mirror, because I put myself together very well and look like the picture of confidence.

When all the talk of self-love surfaced, I was intrigued because it sounded like a justification for vanity to me. But, of course, it's not; it's about learning to appreciate oneself for both positive and negative things, and it's so much more than treating oneself to a spa day. So, I'm working on that. My best friend gets tired of me complaining about aging and doesn't want to commiserate with me. She thinks I should find something else to do rather than focus on myself."

Joanne

"Turning sixty was no big deal for me. While I didn't love birthday calendar reminders, I've always taken care and pride in my appearance and figured I could get away with looking in my late fifties for years to come, for an indefinite amount of time. I used makeup and cosmetic procedures to look as young as possible because in my view, looking young made me feel young. And in feeling young I felt that I was communicating energy and sex appeal.

But that all changed for me as I approached my late sixties. The procedures didn't work as well, the results were less obvious, and I was spending a fortune on my face when I should have focused my finances on other priorities.

I'd recently retired and the rationale of making up my face based on the idea of my identity—how I was viewed by the people I worked with every day—was no longer justified in my mind. Frankly, I was also getting tired of the daily struggle with makeup, fake eyelashes, all kinds of visual tricks to look young, plus the reapplications of makeup at work. And then there were the monthly or quarterly appointments with people wearing scrubs wielding needles, applying serums, and operating lasers, all the machinery and equipment, and having to take vacation days to recover from a face peel or procedure.

Was it all worth it? Yes, at the time, but I'm aware of the negative comments, from my mother, for example, about older women who wore makeup and had surgical procedures, who, in her view, were trying too hard to be someone they were not.

'Who does she think she is?' my mother would snort. This was the comment I remember the most and today, if my mother were alive, I would have responded, 'She is just herself, Mom, no one else.'

I would like to be bare-faced and beautiful but I don't love my bare face. It's blotchy, and the surface of my skin is not as smooth as I want it to be, which is a shame as I've spent a lot of money on trying to improve my skin. These days, I've settled on a concealer, a sun protection foundation, eyebrow pencil, and a little blush. I would use mascara but I don't have many eyelashes left. And tinted lip gloss. That's it. Take me as I am. And if run into any of my old colleagues, and they don't recognize me, so be it. I'm this version of myself now, not the earlier model they knew."

Sherri

"These are the four words to remember about an aging face: retreating, drooping, sagging and wrinkling. My face is a combination of all four of these events, although every cosmetologist that I've consulted with has a more delicate vocabulary, these four words are inescapable. My forehead looks larger because my hairline has changed. The tip of my nose and both of my earlobes are drooping. The fat in my face has moved around and is heading towards my chin and neck. And then there are wrinkles, fine lines, and deep grooves. I can pay lots of money to change all of this or just live with it and get on with doing something else with my life."

There's a reason hairdressing services are offered to women in retirement homes, where many women have standing weekly appointments. The world feels right if Mom is able to get her hair down once or twice a week. Hair represents identity, confirmation of a version of self in which hair is cut and colored in a certain style. We all have friends who cut, style, and color their hair in ways that may seem odd to us, but as each of us sees only what we want to see in the mirror, we have no judgment line to stand upon.

Hair, and specifically hairstyles, represent identity for women just about everywhere. Ask any woman who has a wardrobe of wigs. Hair as identity is the reason that when women are told of the protocols that are part of a cancer treatment, they worry immediately about hair loss. *Who am I if I do not have my hair?* Being bald, unless it is a deliberate statement, is something most women do not want to face. To many, hair loss means being bare and exposed. To other women, baldness signals freedom from the self-imposed burden of doing their hair or living with other people's expectations.

We may consider hair as coverage for many internal anxieties. In confessions shared only with people who cut hair for a living, many women worry about the shape of their head and have their hair cut to conceal flaws, real or imagined, they would be embarrassed for others to see.

Grey hair and thinning hair are reminders of the change in identity that is represented by aging. While some women embrace gray hair and often change their style accordingly, other women fight for years to preserve their hair color.

In previous decades, women who wore their hair long after turning forty were seen as bohemian and eccentric, as if there was something wanton and irresponsible in their decision to let their hair grow. In their sixties, they may still get asked, "When are you going to cut your hair?"—as if there was a rule somewhere that dictates that women over a certain age should not have long hair.

Over the last hundred years women who cut their hair short have been viewed as "looking like a man." We may laugh at the absurdity of those views now, but at the time, women were making statements of self-identity. We're doing the same thing today, but with less judgment.

When I was in my twenties, working as a journalist, an article that I'd written about body image and how we never see ourselves as other people see us was published in a magazine. The most memorable take-aways from the interviews I conducted were from three women, all older.

The oldest woman, then in her early sixties, still had her hair 'done' twice a week, swept up into a tall shape on her head. She told me that having her hair styled this way made her feel taller, more secure, and therefore more powerful in the senior role she played at her office. She saw her hair as a component of her authority. One day, she got caught in a torrential rainstorm and her hair was plastered to her head, the tall shape flattened. After she'd checked herself out in the restroom, she left the building for the rest of the day, unable to face everyone with a different version of herself than the one she carefully contrived around her hair style.

The other two women discussed clothes. One woman, a senior editor at a magazine, and a plus size, told me that she liked to wear dresses in large colorful prints because visually the prints defined the space she occupied in a room and that gave her more confidence. "It keeps people away,'" she told me, "I need my space."

Claire, a radio show host in her early sixties, confessed to owning three wardrobes: for fat days, thin days, and days in between. These were clothes that no one could see given her job behind a microphone, but clothes that reflected her confidence level.

Body image issues may be unresolved from a time that dates back to our teens, but they linger into our sixties, after childbirth, and health issues that indicate medications with profound side effects on appearance, such as weight gain. Judgment around physical attributes, about shape and weight are cruel, and we inflict this often not so silent cruelty on ourselves as well as others. Women see themselves as too fat, too thin, lacking in some places and bulging in others, regretting the shape of their legs, arms, ankles, knees, breasts, calves, or torso.

But if this outward shell that wraps us can be changed and reconstructed, just like our faces, that doesn't necessarily change how we feel.

Amanda

"Dressing myself in my sixties was a completely new challenge. And that was everyday dressing, before I started dating. My waist, long the focus of my style, had disappeared. I didn't go 'in' at the sides, so the shirts I could once tuck in were no longer an option. Getting dressed for those first few dates was far more anxiety-making than it should have been. I worried that my neckline was too low, my skirt was too short, and my tummy was spilling over my pants or skirt. I knew my good physical attributes as well as the parts of me that I liked less, but my clothes did not seem to relate to the body I was now inhabiting."

Kathy

"The thing I hate the most about aging is all the fleshiness that has appeared over the years. There just seems to be so much, well, extra flesh. Dressing is an issue. How much flesh to reveal and how much to conceal. There is extra flesh on my face, and I can deal with that but struggle with what to wear to conceal the extra flesh around my knees, on the back of my arms and back, around my shoulders, and on my inner thighs, and I'm not even overweight."

—❧—

Rebecca

"I have become unremarkable. I just want someone to acknowledge me, to say I look pretty. I'm not expecting anyone to tell me that I look 'young,' but even 'nice' would do, I'd settle for 'nice.' Even when I dress up or pay special attention to myself and no one says anything, my friends or family (I've given up expecting a response from my husband), I feel that they're not seeing the same me, the me that I see in the mirror. Have I changed that much?

Do they see my age before the effort that I've put into to looking good? Or, and this is my fear, do people see me as an older person trying to compensate for my age by fitting in, carefully organizing myself to draw attention away from the signs of aging on my face and in my body, and therefore I have become part of the background, like the piece of furniture that is always in the same place?"

M. J.

"I had lost weight before, but later in life it seemed like doing it again was too high a mountain to climb. I couldn't even think about getting to base camp. In addition to physical health issues and over-thinking, the activities of over-eating and over-drinking became the norm, and by my late fifties and early sixties I'd gained eighty pounds.

Something happened that proved to be the jolt I needed. After experiencing severe chest pains, I was diagnosed with plaque round my heart. Over the last year I've become a regular at the gym, another thing I never thought that I'd do, and I've made myself eat and drink less. I've lost fifty pounds and regained physical activities I thought were lost for good.

I look at men on the running machines at the gym and I no longer worry as I wobble away doing my walking. I look at slim young women and no longer worry that I've lost that. We are all on our journey. This is my new mantra."

Karen

"Over the last decade, particularly, I feel that I've faded into the background and become a shadow of myself. This is what I feared most of all being in my sixties and approaching my seventies. That it's all over, in a way, and that the remaining years are those of increasing infirmity, anxiety about maintaining mental faculties, and the onset of physical limitations.

As we age, we women, it's as if we've slipped silently into a room and settled into a quiet corner, unnoticed. The world goes on around us while we sit patiently on the sidelines, waiting our turn.

Recently, I've decided that waiting isn't good enough for me. For as long as I'm still agile I'm going to live my best life and that's going to involve an attitude shift on my part."

Chapter Sixteen

Love in all its guises

C heck out any online forum or social media platform for and about women in their sixties, and aside from the questions, mostly asked and answered, about health, pensions, and cosmetics procedures, many of the posts are about love. How to find it, how to keep it, revive it, and maintain it, and what to do if it gets lost, particularly if the closest, most intimate relationship has spluttered and burnt out. Love has many guises: love for children, for parents, for spouses, for friends, for old loves and for new loves, and for significant others.

Does love become more complicated as we age? Do we think it should become less complicated? Although there is no reason to think that we may care less, perhaps we care more, and therefore, potentially hurt more, in understanding love. Has our love overwhelmed some and our definition of love pushed away others?

For many women, our sixties is a time of making peace with love, and perhaps learning to compromise with love or redefine it—even live without it. There may be more people in our lives—stepchildren, daughters- and sons-in-law, and grandchildren—and more complications and situations to navigate. We may be overflowing with love, or our feelings of love may have capsized and now have considerable constraints where we once saw endless opportunities.

Friends change. It is said that proximity is a key component to maintaining friendship, and in the gulf that distance creates, we gravitate toward other people, not to replace old friendships but to enjoy and explore new relationships on a practical level, with people who are physically close by.

Love means loss and by the time we are in our sixties we may be familiar with both experiences and the emotions may have a sense of repetition. And we may have encountered new love and new lives. In the process we may have been required to reinvent ourselves, multiple times, adapt to new ways of living—and loving—and find new people to populate our lives. Love is always complicated, never simple. No one ever talks about a simple love.

Chapter Seventeen

Dee

Reconciling with estrangement

Dee wonders that if she had to be assessed as a parent, as a mother, she might only receive a passing grade. She feels guilty about the decisions she made and is seeking to reconcile with her daughter. She also wonders if sometimes parents and children are mismatched.

"When I told my mother that I planned to divorce my husband and move into an apartment with our only daughter, who was then eight years old, she said, 'Oh, so you're planning to bring up my granddaughter in a broken home.'

It was one of the few times that I can remember arguing with my mother. We always got along well and we were close, seeing eye to eye on most things. We'd been best friends when I was growing up, probably because my father died when I was quite young, and I was an only child. I challenged her broken home comment because I could think of many intact homes, with both parents present in the house, that were structurally broken with just the veneer of being intact. It felt as if my mother was judging and condemning all single parents as bad parents.

We talked about it and she apologized, and she subsequently supported my decision and worked to maintain a relationship with my ex-husband, which was helpful to Livia, our daughter. My mother and Livia were close, and it was wonderful for me to see my mother so relaxed with Livia as I didn't recall her being that way with me. But my mother passed last year, and I think the reason for my current introspection is that I miss her.

Now I'm in my late sixties, and I work part-time. My daughter is in her early thirties. I've been thinking a lot about the last two decades. I don't have a good relationship with my daughter.

Livia's father, my ex-husband, and I managed a workable arrangement after our divorce, resolving our differences so that we could care for Livia although as he traveled a lot for his job, I was Livia's primary caregiver. Her father got married and he and his new wife had children—twins, two boys—so Livia has two stepbrothers she loves, although they are ten years younger than her.

I got remarried, but to a man who could not have children. Livia never warmed to her stepfather, although he tried, especially helping her with homework, but she maintained that they had nothing in common and resented him. I met my husband at the university where I worked in the admissions department and he was a lecturer. Livia was a teenager by the time I got married, not interested in homework or academics, and especially not interested in us, so it wasn't easy.

In her mid-teens Livia found a group of kids outside of her classmates. She started sneaking out at night and sleeping with boys. It was a challenge to get her to complete school and apply for college. We argued a great deal. There were a lot of slammed doors and tears. I never did any of that sort of thing with my mother, and I struggled to understand my daughter. My husband and I let out a sigh of relief when Livia left for college.

At one point, Livia wanted to go and live with her father and his young family. She spent a lot of time at her father's house, got on well with her stepmother, and always wanted to spend holidays there. Now I realize that it would've been better for her if she'd moved in with them. Their house was a noisy, easy-going environment, never tidy, in my opinion, but Livia preferred that to the house of 'two old people reading books every night,' as she described my husband and myself; 'a house,' she said, 'where everything has to be kept in place all the time.' It's true that I like things to be neat and tidy, and put away when not in use, and it's true that Livia's room was always a mess. She's a disorganized person, just like her father.

I was unwilling to let Livia go and live with her father's family because I felt it would be signaling to everyone that

I'd failed as a mother, unable to have my daughter live with me. At the time, my excuse was that she would be a burden on a young family. There were many fights about this, but I stood my ground.

Recently, I've reflected on the idea that this decision was less about Livia than it was about me. It was what worked for me, not what was in Livia's best interests—and her father's family would have made her feel welcome— and I feel ashamed because I didn't put her first; I put me first.

Livia left for college and she's never been home again. When she comes back to town, she stays with her father so she can spend time with her stepbrothers, and I see her on holidays such as Thanksgiving. We have occasional phone calls during the year that are uncomfortable for both of us. She told her father, who told me, that I don't understand her. She feels that her teenage years were all about me wanting her to be someone she could never be, doing things I wanted because I expected her to be like me. According to my ex-husband, Livia told him that she was never interested in being the perfect daughter and didn't even like reading that much.

She's evasive, or maybe defensive, when I ask her about her life. She says she is happy; she works several jobs and shares a house with a group of friends. That is not the career path or the life I wanted for her. She once told me, 'You want too much for me, Mom; you want me to be like you, with the same expectations in life, and you're always worried about what people will think, and how you will be judged.'

I sent her money during, and after, she left college, and bought her gifts, until several people pointed out, including my husband, that I was sending her money and buying her things to feel better about myself. She rarely said thank you, and it was explained to me that this was Livia's way of sending me a message that she didn't want my gifts or my money.

As a parent, I don't think it's wrong to want certain things for your children, to have hopes for them, to try and guide them in certain directions, but I have to face the fact that I have a failed relationship with my daughter because we are so different, and that it should be on me to understand her and not the other way around.

While I hate to admit it, Livia is not the daughter I'd planned for, and from what she tells her father, I'm not the mother she wanted. She maintains that I couldn't accept her for who she is, and I'm always judging her because I make suggestions all the time, hints as to how she could be living or improving her life. I'm just trying to help. I've also wondered from time to time if parents and children can be mismatched.

I don't want to go into my seventies with a strained relationship with my only child. I feel that I need to tell her that I accept responsibility for my actions and apologize to her for how her teenage years turned out. Even though

Livia has said, and done, things to me that have been very hurtful, my husband says that I'll only embarrass her if I confront her, and that I shouldn't expect too much. He advises that I should make peace with myself, rather than try to make peace with my daughter.

I hope that we can find a way to reconcile, before health issues and other age-related events increase the gulf between us. I wonder sometimes, if she would ever come to see me if I ended up in a nursing home? I think about that. If she gets married and has a child, I don't want to be on the outside of her life, looking in. I want to be in her life, now, before it's too late."

Chapter Eighteen

Jennifer

Life after loss

The unexpected loss of her husband changed Jennifer's plans for her sixties. With the love of her life gone, Jennifer is finding ways to reframe her identity for the future without letting go of the past.

"I lost my husband when I was fifty-nine and he was sixty-four, just a few years before he'd planned to retire. He died of a heart attack. There were no warning signs. It just happened.

Turning sixty was like any other year, any other day, week, or month. All I could feel was the loss of the man I loved, my husband, and the father of our daughters. In speaking to other widows, I've found that we'd all shared the same experiences. Each of us had to straighten out affairs, close accounts, and deal with endless paperwork while struggling with overwhelming emotions. Whether our husbands were neat and orderly or pack rats, these men were living as if they didn't plan to die.

I still feel robbed of our time, which could have been spent together in our sixties and beyond, and I am angry. I stopped working part-time in a public-facing job to manage everything that was involved in dealing with my husband's estate, and because I could no longer tolerate the looks of sympathy. It felt as if I was wearing a shirt that was advertising my loss. And coming home from work to an empty house was terrible. It just felt better when I stayed home and didn't leave the house.

In time, I sold my husband's fishing boat and his fishing gear; our daughters are not interested in fishing. Most of the tools in the garage, which, just like his own father, he collected more than he used, found new homes with his male buddies. I gave his clothes away—although that was very hard, and I finally broke down and let a good friend help me. I thought I could manage alone, but I was wrong. In time, I rearranged the bedroom and the bathroom to no longer have 'his' and 'hers' sides to anything, just 'hers.'

His large reclining chair in the living room was an accusation that I was alive and he was not. It was where he'd spent a great deal of time, but the chair did not comfort me; other than me curling up in it and sobbing after he died. Its place in the living room was a reminder of his absence. My daughters protested, but they didn't live at home and didn't have to sit on the sofa in the evening, in front of the TV, with the empty chair next to them. I gave the chair away, and I'm considering getting new furniture.

In trying to cope with the guilt that I'd survived and he had not, I finally sought help and now go to therapy. I'm still not at the point where I can go through all the photographs of us, of us as a family together. The box of photographs sits under the bed, and I feel like a broody hen sleeping over it and keeping it safe, but there is no date for when I plan to open it.

Most couples at this stage in life, in their sixties, are on the path to fulfilling the plans they'd made in the previous decade. They talk about their plans, at length: where they're going, with whom, and what they're going to see and do. Had my husband lived, we would have been doing the same thing. We'd often discussed the bucket list of trips we wanted to take, but taking those trips alone was not something I wanted to do.

As friends began retiring in their sixties, the differences between us were painfully obvious. These friends had partners and spouses, and even if the marriage was not great, there was still someone, a companion, a friend, someone, to share the plans. Being invited to join couples on trips was a short-lived experience, and that was down to my mood.

I began to resent people who were openly affectionate. I had no one to cuddle with, no one to hold my hand, no one to touch and no one to touch me. I was always the odd number at a dinner table. I had to reframe my new identity and understand that, as kind and well-intentioned as our friends were, I needed to extract myself from the group, and part ways with more than a few of our coupled friends. I stay close to the wives in the group but rarely see all the couples together anymore.

As everyone knows, finding new friends when you are older is difficult. I met a widower by accident in a coffee shop, and we started chatting. We didn't plan on turning our coffee meetings into anything that resembled a relationship, but we had a lot to share, to commiserate over. I didn't know his wife, and he didn't know my husband, and the anonymity seemed to work for us because sympathy for someone you've never met can only go so far. I really think that we helped each other, a little bit like therapy, I suppose. But one day he told me that he'd met a woman, and as he was eager to begin a new relationship, our coffee meetings ended.

There's that saying that as one door closes, another one opens. I'm not only unable but unwilling to close the door on the chapter of my life with the love of my life, but other doors have opened. I still think of my husband every single day. Something reminds me, something someone says, or a memory of him is triggered, and there are always, always, things that I want to share with him.

I'm trying to lean into the future, but it's difficult not to resent the overwhelming sense of loss and disappointment that has been my experience so far of my sixties."

Chapter Nineteen

Shelley

Dating after sixty

Dating at any age is daunting, but for Shelley, who after divorcing in her sixties threw herself into finding a companion, dating was a challenge in ways she had never imagined.

"People say they are 'just looking' when they start dating, like browsing online, but that's not true. We're all on a mission to find someone, a partner, maybe a future spouse. I don't remember much of dating in my twenties, it was all very confusing, but I eventually found someone, fell in love, got married, and now after twenty-five years, we're divorced. The difference between dating back then and now is that people are concerned about how much time there's left to spend with someone.

I'm sixty-four years old and in good health. I could live another twenty-five years. The man I meet could also be in his sixties and live another twenty years. Or not. He might sicken shortly after we became a permanent item, and then

I'd be a nursemaid. I shouldn't think like that, but this thought pops into my head when I'm out on a date.

If you think I'm getting ahead of myself, bear with me. Another way to look at dating in your sixties, one that I adopted early on, particularly if the goal is to cohabit at some point, is to look for a companion that you wouldn't mind looking after one day and wouldn't object to if he had to care for you. It's surprising how things can change on a date when you think, as you look across the table at a man, *'Would I like this man to change my diapers?'* or *'Would I be okay changing his diapers?'"*

I wish, but now know better, that I'll just find someone to fall in love with where we are blind to what the future holds for both of us. Common sense tells me that one of us is going to have to care for the other, and—here is another sobering thought— potentially look after the other person's family members, if there's an elderly parent who is still alive and needs care, for instance, or dependent children. People are right when they say that dating in your older years is about dating other people's baggage.

Somewhere over the decades of being married and divorced, I've lost a part of myself, the part that was tied to my identity of what I looked like—or, I should say, what I used to look like. It doesn't help that my body has changed shape; it's thickened and there are fewer curves, and I'm just bulkier than before. Much as I hate to admit it, I relate to the comment that women become 'boxy' in shape as they age. And I resent that. It's not as if we don't have to cope with all the other issues associated with aging. Choosing a dating wardrobe was very difficult.

Finding someone to date was a struggle. I had to learn how to find my way around dating sites and get used to a new language with multiple hidden meanings, and different expectations on both sides. My friends couldn't help—they were all married or determinedly single, and some just said they'd given up hope.

And although in movies children help their parents navigate dating sites, my son and daughter were horrified that I might present them with a stepdad one day and an entirely new family to blend into, at a time when my daughter was getting married and my son had become engaged. So, they weren't any help.

All I want is companionship, someone to go out to dinner with, attend an event with, or just take walks in the park together, but I quickly learned not to discuss my dating life with either of my children and I never introduced them to anyone because, after almost a year of trying, I never met anyone I wanted my children to meet.

I would get excited about initial phone calls with a potential new man, only to learn that he spent every weekend on his hobbies or that his adult children still lived at home. I've been rejected for all these reasons: I don't go to church enough, or I attend too many services; I like the beach (this by a man with a history of skin cancer, so I understand this rejection); I don't like reptiles (so not happy with pet snakes); I like to eat dinner early and not late; I drink alcohol; I've never been fishing and I'm not interested in learning how to clean a fish. And then, of course, there are deep political convictions that are definitely deal breakers.

Men who had been widowed were often more eager to get remarried than those who had been divorced. Men who have been married before are often looking for someone to fill the shoes of their wife, someone with similar habits and lifestyle, even dress style! These dates were like job interviews. Did I cook every night? Did I do my own cleaning, or employ a housekeeper? Did I have any health issues? Had I made a will? How long would I continue to work? And the most offensive conversations of all were steered towards pensions and savings with hints that I should reveal whether I could sustain myself financially. On a second date!

Of course, I had a few questions of my own. I wanted to read between the lines to find out if the man was kind or not, what his political views were (on this topic I found an easy get-out-of-a-date-quick-card by announcing that I'd voted for the opposite party—although it might have been a lie, sometimes I was desperate to leave the date), and a list of attributes I'd written down on a piece of paper in case I forgot them. I left the list in the ladies' bathroom of a restaurant once, and a helpful server handed it to me at the dinner table—in front of my date. Happily, he thought it was funny, and I wondered, for a minute, if we might have a connection after all, but that minute passed.

I've sat over one too many drinks with someone I was trying my hardest to rationalize liking. 'Not too bad' is not encouraging enough, and by the end of the first drink can become 'not good enough,' and that's common to both parties. I'm okay not being good enough for someone if they aren't good enough for me.

Dating in your sixties isn't fun. It's more like a business negotiation than dating as I remember it. If you can get past the initial conversations where both parties are trying to find common ground, count the children and grand-children while mentally making note of how many more people one would have in a new life with this person, the next topics are politics, religion, and social values which can turn a potential date into a non-starter in a sentence.

Who pays for dinner, by the way? One man was turned off by the car I drive, and more than one man saw my inde-pendence in spending vacations with a group of girlfriends as a threat. There are men who are wary of women they call gold-diggers, and women who are wary of men who do not have enough money to support their retirement and are looking for an affluent wife. A 'nurse with a purse' is the description.

I know women who've met and married men while in their sixties, but these men are often in their seventies or even early eighties, slower, hard of hearing, less mobile, with some health issues and they're settled in their ways—ways they expect a woman to adapt to. I'm guessing that both people decided that they'd be willing to change each other's diapers one day. At this point I haven't met anyone I'd be willing to nurse, who doesn't need a purse, but I'm still hoping."

Chapter Twenty

Nicola

Divergent paths

After twenty years of marriage, Nicola retired and discovered that all the things that had once worked in the relationship for her now no longer seemed viable or even desirable.

"**M**y husband and I were both in our forties when we got married, each for the first time. We don't have children and therefore we won't have grandchildren. We both have siblings with children and grandchildren, but they live across the country and we don't see them often and we aren't close. I can't be enthusiastic with my friends who have grandchildren. I have nothing to add to any of the conversations, but I don't regret my decision not to have children.

I've had an extremely satisfying working life, a career that I started building in my twenties and one in which I broke a few glass ceilings. I'm very proud of myself and often wish my parents were still alive to witness what I've accomplished. The positions I've held always involved travel, usually to distant parts of the world, as the contracts had to be executed in person, and I was often away for weeks at a time.

My husband is a technical editor and he's always worked from home. As I traveled the globe, he was always there for me at the end of a trip, at the airport to pick me up—even though the company I worked for would have paid for a taxi for me—with a welcome home meal on the table. He took care of running the house and paying the bills, which would have gone into arrears as I struggled to keep track of time zones when traveling. He was my emotional rock, patient, supportive, and reliable, as I unloaded all my stress and tension at the end of a work trip. He's also the primary caretaker of our two cats who completely ignore me at this point.

At sixty-five years old, late last year, I retired. My husband is two years older than I am and he still works, although it's part-time. He spends every day in his office upstairs, just as he's always done, in a room I never enter. My husband smokes, and although he keeps a window open, I don't like to go into the room. Everything smells of smoke. He even keeps clothes to change into (in a plastic bag) in his office because he knows that emerging from the fug of the room, in clothes that smell of smoke, is offensive to me. I imagine that when I was traveling, he didn't bother to change his clothes.

Thanks to my well-paying jobs, we've been able to pay off our mortgage and we've saved a lot of money over the years. Now, I want to spend some of that money, as well as use up all my hotel and airline points and miles, on traveling together. We've talked about it over the years, when I would describe places I visited, places I'd like to return to and share with him because I think he'd like them. And while he always seemed interested, we never made any plans.

Now I want to make plans and he is resistant. He doesn't seem to be listening to me, and I've realized something that I never wanted to recognize before; and that my husband's addiction to tobacco means that he doesn't want to fly, and definitely not on a long-haul flight to a distant continent. But honestly, it would be difficult to get him on a two-hour flight to anywhere because he'd be anxious about a flight delay. A four-hour delay on the tarmac at an airport, for instance, would mean he couldn't smoke.

When I suggest nicotine patches, hypnotherapy, and anything else I can think of so that we can take a trip together, he reminds me that he tried all these solutions before, when he was in his forties, and they didn't work.

He doesn't want to find a cure for his nicotine dependence. Nicotine is a big part of his life, and being a smoker is part of his identity, even though he knows it's offensive to most people, he sees no reason to change. When I point out that his cough is getting worse and I can hear him wheezing, he just shrugs. He fears going to the doctor as the visit would involve listening to his chest and he is terrified of getting lung cancer. It's been years since he had an annual check-up. I can't understand how he seems to be healthy when he rarely exercises and smokes so many cigarettes.

At this point we're at a stand-off. To fill my new-found time after retirement I managed a landscape project for our garden, which we'd both neglected for years; I lacked time and my husband lacked interest. As part of this renovation the landscape company created a gazebo close to the house where we can cook outside or just sit and have a drink in the evening. But with a drink, my husband automatically lights a cigarette, the first of many, and because the cigarettes are now symbols of what is preventing us from traveling, I detest them.

I'm married to a man who doesn't want to do much more than keep his routines, and, work daily in his office, where he can smoke. I'm not sure how many jobs he is working on, and we don't need the money. He values his private time, although he could be looking at porn for all I know. It's always been that way; it's just when I was working, I didn't want to see it.

There's a good chance that smoking will eventually have an impact on his health and that I'll be looking after him, helping attach him to breathing equipment. I know that he'd be there for me if I became sick and incapacitated—between trips outside the hospital to smoke. A thought occurred to me the other day: *Do retirement homes take in chronic smokers?* But before all that happens, I want to enjoy everything we have accomplished individually and together and travel and share the world with him, but without cigarettes, and I feel as if he's choosing his addiction over me.

I'm healthy. I'm trying to find things to do by myself. Some of my friends are widows and could travel with me, but after decades of traveling alone I want to share adventures with my husband—but his depression, which he also does not acknowledge, and his addiction to nicotine, prevent this from happening. One of my friends suggested that I think of my husband as a disabled person, and to act as if I'm living with a person with a disability, but that doesn't really help.

This isn't the life I imagined for myself. Am I paying the price for all those years I traveled the world, working to fill my dreams of career and chase monetary success? His dreams are small. He wants his routine and the freedom to smoke. My dreams are big, they've always been big, and I'm frustrated by the limitations he's imposed on himself, and on us. I don't know what the answer is, but I hope that we can find it sooner rather than later."

Jodi

"Do all marriages end up this way? We're happy enough, know each other well, but the spark disappeared a long time ago. I don't think either of us have the energy to change anything. We are companions, friends, confidantes, and both love spending time with our grandchildren. Our children are important to us. I suppose that is how things just work out. I would say that of all our friends, only a handful are still crazy about each other in ways that just make me feel uncomfortable to watch. I guess I find it difficult to believe them, or maybe I am envious."

Chapter Twenty-One

Lori J. Bridges-Hahn

Dreams come true

Lori's story is one of love for a soulmate who was unattainable until, after several marriages and divorces (on both sides) and almost two decades, she and her soulmate were free to be together. In Lori's view, true love is still possible in your sixties and it compensates for the aches and pains of aging. After several tumultuous decades, she writes that her sixties have brought her more joy than she has ever known.

"Recently, my husband and I adopted an eight-week-old kitten from a local rescue operated from a two-story house built in the late 1800s. We asked about seeing the available kittens and were told that the kittens were housed on the second floor.

As I eyed the narrow, uneven stairs, a deep groan escaped...the groan was filled with dread at the challenge I faced. My arthritic knees ached as I grabbed the railing and pulled my overweight body up each step, slowly ascending to the top. Several minutes later, my husband and I were both relieved to be back on the first floor. We would only face the two steps onto our porch at home and then we would be in our house. (And yes, we did adopt a kitten—an orange and white monster we named Charlie!)

This situation is just another in a long list of similar challenges that I have experienced since turning sixty nearly five years ago. Lack of a good night's sleep (thank you, bladder, for filling up so quickly), an inability to lose more than twenty pounds (no matter how much I kill myself at the gym or doing Zumba), a total knee replacement, and arthritis in my hands (coupled with carpal tunnel syndrome) often have me wondering, *If I'm this bad at sixty-five, how am I going to manage in another ten years?*

But then I recall all the other significant decades of my life and, quite honestly, I'm thrilled to be where I am now in my sixties. My childhood and teen years were fraught with teasing and bullying. My twenties and thirties were spent in a loveless, disappointing marriage. The only good thing to come from twenty years of misery was the adoption of my beautiful daughter, Rachel (who will be thirty-three this year).

The year I turned forty I fell in love with my soulmate, Doug. The relationship was doomed from the start. He and I were both married to other people at the time (yes, I admit it, and although I'm not proud of it, it was what we both needed and what I especially needed to improve my self-esteem). Sadly, the relationship did not last. After five months, we went back to our respective spouses. I ended up leaving my husband for good the following year and met someone else right away.

During my forties I divorced, remarried, and maintained a close bond with my daughter during her teen years. During this decade I also experienced the loss of my mother.

But I continued to see Doug, the man I'd broken up with, the man I considered to be my soulmate, until I was in my mid-forties. He was a guitarist/vocalist in my best friend's band, and I attended many gigs during those years, so many that I have lost count. Doug and I talked now and then at the gigs, and every time I drove away, headed for home with my new husband (or with a friend who had joined me), the tears welled in my eyes as I realized how much I missed Doug, and I knew that I still loved him even though at the time we were both married to other people.

My fifties brought my daughter's graduation from high school and her journey to college. During my fifties, Doug's band broke up, the band I loved so much and with this break-up I no longer saw him. In my fifties I also started my own business. After spending decades as an executive administrative assistant, I opened a business as a wedding planner but shuttered that company several years later to follow my passion for writing, first publishing a book of poetry and subsequently several novels.

I was in my fifties when I lost my father and, shortly after Dad passed, my husband changed drastically. Once a heavy drinker and drug addict, he'd been sober for nearly twenty years, but somewhere along the way, he'd become angry, temperamental, and even violent. Four months after I turned fifty-eight, he attacked me and threatened me with a loaded gun. He was out of his mind that entire day, and I chalked it up as a result of his liver disease and a bout of encephalopathy—a condition that can often alter a person's behavior and personality, even to the point of violence. After a nine-day stay in the hospital, my husband came home.

The next few months were quiet but strained. But once my husband began to verbally abuse me again, and threatened to harm me, I contacted my attorney and began divorce proceedings.

In the meantime, I happened across Doug's Facebook page. Doug the guitarist, the love of my life, and my soulmate, posted that his wife of twenty-five years had died. I couldn't believe it. I fretted for a couple of days and then decided to privately message him. It had been fifteen years since we'd last seen each other at a gig, and nineteen years since we'd been involved with each other. I kept my message simple but heartfelt...one of sympathy, and condolence, and I offered my hand in friendship.

Doug and I chatted online a few times. As the divorce from my second husband was in the process of being finalized, I messaged Doug and asked if he would like to meet for lunch. At the time, we lived an hour apart, but he finally agreed and I drove to his town, picked him up at his apartment, and we went to lunch. I knew as soon as our eyes met that I was still in love with him. I went into his apartment after lunch, and we chatted for a couple of hours, comparing our lives and all that had happened to us during our fifteen-year separation.

It was when we stood as I prepared to leave that he said to me, 'Come here, you," and opened his arms to pull me into his embrace. This was not just a hug between friends; it was tender and loving, and neither of us wanted it to end. Within a few days, we confessed to each other that the feelings we'd shared in the past were still there, and as strong as ever.

After my divorce was finalized, I married Doug. Now, we own a home together which we share with a new kitten, Charlie. I can say that my sixties, for me, are the best years of my life. I was reunited with the man who was meant for me all along, and I am finally in a marriage that doesn't involve disappointment, loneliness, or verbal or physical abuse.

Doug and I travel to the Smoky Mountains and to a friend's lake house in Indiana, and we enjoy country dri-ves, music, games, and cards with our friends, and just being together. My body hurts and it's hard to walk. My hands don't work as well as they used to. I get tired easily and cannot lose weight no matter how hard I try. But my sixties have also brought more joy and happiness than I have ever known.

Based on my experience, I believe that it is never too late to make your dreams come true, friends are everything, and true love is still possible. All these things make the aches and pains of getting older so much easier to bear. Life is a treasure and a gift, and I am living it to the fullest."

Lori J. Bridges-Hahn, Ohio, USA

Chapter Twenty-Two

Linda

Grandparenting

On the verge of retirement, the unexpected arrival of a grandchild upended Linda's carefully planned future. She found herself embarking on parenting for the second time in her life.

"When our son was nineteen, he and his then girlfriend had a child, a little girl whom they named Destiny. After taking a year off after high school to gain work experience before heading to college, our son, Clark, was ill-equipped to look after a child, and his plans to go to college had to be shelved while the immediate needs to care for a baby was addressed.

For a while, Clark and his girlfriend, Nicole, lived with Nicole's parents, but this arrangement didn't last for long. Nicole fought constantly with her parents, and there were two younger siblings living in the house. It was crowded and Nicole didn't seem to get along with anyone, and Clark found living on her parents' sofa to be challenging.

He was never sure who would look after Destiny while he was at work.

Making minimum wage, Clark could barely afford an apartment and Nicole didn't work and seemed to have no interest in finding a job, claiming that childcare was too expensive for what she could make in income. We didn't disagree, but Nicole's attitude didn't sit well with us.

Steve, Clark's father, and I, never really liked Nicole, although we'd only really met her a few times, but we tried for Clark's sake to get along with her. Clark wasn't in love with Nicole and the pregnancy wasn't planned. We helped out financially, by paying a deposit and the first month's rent on an apartment, but what started out as occasionally giving him checks here and there, eventually turned into us paying for the rent in full every month on his apartment. We also bought clothes and diapers for Destiny, which we were happy to do. Steve was still working full-time and I was working part-time, but we began to wonder if we would need to extend our working lives if we were going to be involved in raising our granddaughter.

Things changed when Nicole became pregnant again, and this time the father was not Clark. Now Steve and I felt sure that all our plans for retirement would be upended, but we didn't know how. And we were right. Clark would bring Destiny over to see us, and she would stay for longer and longer while he worked as many shifts as he could. With news of another man in Nicole's life, Clark was reluctant to continue providing for Nicole—but he didn't want to abandon his daughter.

One day, Nicole moved out of her parents' home and took Destiny with her. Clark would attempt to see Destiny, but Nicole blocked many of his efforts, or she would want to drop off Destiny for a few hours unscheduled when Clark was due at work. Sometimes, hours turned into days, or a weekend. Clark would reach out to us to help him so that he could continue to work and not lose his job. Every time Nicole dropped off Destiny, the signs of neglect were unmistakable, and we voiced our concerns to Clark. Destiny would arrive in dirty clothes, in need of a bath, without diapers, formula or food, a change of clothes, or any toys.

Things came to a head when several of Clark's friends saw Nicole out at night, in bars, with her new boyfriend, and with Destiny, now about six months old, in tow. Clark tracked Nicole down through her parents, who hadn't seen their daughter for weeks and had washed their hands of her, but who guessed approximately where she might be living. Clark found his baby daughter living in something that he said resembled a squat, where drugs and alcohol were evident, and it broke his heart.

He came to us, humiliated, in tears, regretful but deeply anxious about Destiny and asked us if we could help. While Steve and I were worried for Clark and Destiny, we thought—in truth, hoped—that somehow, all this would resolve itself. We were fortunate that we had savings to help pay for things, but having a child, a baby, living full-time with us, was another matter. But just like Clark, we found it intolerable that Destiny was being raised in such an irresponsible manner.

Clark involved the authorities, who removed Destiny from Nicole, and then over the months that followed we became involved and sponsored Destiny. Our case was helped by the fact that Nicole's parents wanted no part of their daughter or their grandchild, especially with a second grandchild on the way. As it stands now, Destiny lives with us. We've converted Clark's old bedroom into a nursery and renovated the basement so that Clark can live in it. It's pretty bare bones, but Clark isn't asking for anything else. His goal is to work and start college part-time. He's committed to raising his daughter but he cannot do so without our help.

There's always a chance that Nicole will attempt to remove Destiny from our home, but given how she spends her time, it's unlikely that she'll be able to provide a stable and safe environment for her daughter.

So here we are, in our mid-sixties, being parents again, this time to a little girl. I left my job to care for Destiny full-time. I take her out in her stroller to coffee shops and parks but have little in common with the other mothers, who are all decades younger than me. We will enroll her in day care, in time, because I'll need to find part-time work to help pay for day care and we're hoping that through day care we can meet other parents, other children. We haven't started to think about schools yet but will need to.

Some of our friends have become grandparents, but the difference is that they hand their grandchildren back after a few hours. We bring Destiny home with us.

Steve and I have postponed all the trips we planned for our retirement, for now. Clark has a week's vacation coming up and we will use that time to take a trip, just Steve and I, to somewhere on our bucket list, but we've abandoned thoughts of selling the house and moving. Clark grew up in this house, it is mostly paid for, and now it will become a place to raise another child. As much as we love Destiny and Clark, it's hard not to feel resentment. Our friends are starting to enjoy their retirement and we're still changing diapers day and night, and our life revolves around the baby's schedule.

But this is love—not the love we'd planned for our son, not the love we'd planned to give or receive but this is what love looks like in our lives today. And if we can give this love in our lives, and the chance to our granddaughter, whom we dearly love, to live her best life, that is what life evidently has in store for us."

Angela

"It's safe to say that by now I've checked all the boxes for emotional maturity. I feel that I've done the work on myself that I needed to do before I turned seventy. It's not going to get easier from now on. There was a choice, a time when I could have said, 'I just can't be bothered with any kind of self-reflection. I'll just go on as I am.' But I'm glad that I delved into my recent, and distant, past. Now, I feel ready for my seventies and whatever the decade will bring to me. I've had a great life so far, and I don't see a reason for that to change. But I'm aware that not everyone feels the same way as I do."

Chapter Twenty-Three

If not now, when

I think of my brain as elastic: it needs to be stretched, pulled taut, and released as I explore the world, changing and adapting to new things, and constantly learning as I age.

W omen in their fifties are usually more curious than fearful about what the next decade might hold. But for the transition from sixty to seventy the outlook is different. While some women in their late sixties look with an even, steady gaze at their seventies, reconciled to the view, others find turning seventy to represent something of a precipice, with a future that contains imagined dread and potential future disappointments based on physical limitations.

Transitioning through the decade of their sixties, with time spinning by, women ask questions of themselves. *Did I do enough? Did I accomplish more, or less, than I wanted to? Should I do more in the time that is left to me?*

It is reasonable to think that when we lose a partner, or a friend, after a long or short illness, or unexpectedly, we might reframe our view of time. At least the intention is spoken to do more in the time remaining after the premature demise of a loved one. The reminder of mortality that a funeral or a cremation represents often translates, briefly, into prompts to do more with our remaining time. But loss does not always act as a trigger for encouragement or convert into urgency to accomplish more. Loss may highlight the time remaining, the ticking clock, but our responses may resemble New Year's Resolutions—easily made, and just as easily broken as the demands of everyday continue to be the focus.

Over the years of our lives we retain the same personality traits, at, say, twenty-eight, thirty-six, forty-five, or even fifty-two, although circumstances combined with aging sometimes turn a reckless soul into a more timid, reserved woman, and a more cautious woman into someone who takes unexpected risks in a burst of late-stage energy. In our sixties, if we are open to it, we can reflect on the decade and prepare ourselves for life in the future.

When we take stock of our lives, we are invariably proud of our accomplishments. Yes, there are regrets, but there is also an opportunity to redress the balance. Increasingly, due to the efforts of women bloggers, writers, journalists, and podcasters, in spotlighting the lives of women in their sixties and seventies, aging may be seen more as an adventure, an opportunity to reaffirm that we are still alive, than something to trudge through. A sense of community is promoted and we are encouraged to remove the shackles of our own perceptions of age, inherited from previous generations. We can embrace aging alone or partnered up, but there are two distinct conversations that emerge in our sixties and continue into our seventies, and these are creativity and company.

The default status for women in their sixties and seventies is to lean into their creativity, picking up pursuits they may have abandoned years ago. Women have long been encouraged to take up "granny arts," such as learning or relearning how to sew, crochet, or knit. Older women are depicted as puttering around gardens, volunteering, and taking art, pottery or photography classes. Plenty of younger women do exactly the same thing but there is a different set of rules, a double standard, as to how older women are perceived.

While not all these occupations involve contact with other people, being in the company of others, which we are told is beneficial to us, is better than being alone, sitting in a room with the treachery of our thoughts for company. New people in our lives become late-stage acquaintances, sometimes friends, and often safety nets as we become frail and distance creates barriers for family support.

Creativity is a word usually applied to arts and crafts, but there is creativity in everything we do: in cooking, in "creating" groups, in just about every aspect of life. But what happens to creativity, something that is inside all of us, if we do not pay attention to it? Does is just bottle itself up, yearning for release? Does it lie dormant, because we never saw a purpose for it (*I'm not a creative person,* some women might think) so it doesn't expect to be called upon? Or does creativity, unexplored and unused, curdle inside of us and become rancid, pushing up against us, harming our bodies and brains because we have not given creativity an outlet—any outlet?

We all know people who discovered early on in life a skill for drawing, arranging, painting, sewing, carving, doing something creative, only to suppress it, or have this creativity suppressed over the years due to time or circumstantial constraints. For women in their sixties, there is the now the time and the opportunity to explore, once again, the intention and experience of creative pursuits, and not necessarily in conventional ways. There are local community resources as well as plenty of online opportunities to learn new and different things.

The decade of the sixties provides space to learn and relearn skills, without purpose or consequence, but for the sheer pleasure of learning and creating. There's no judgment except our own which we should know how to deal with by now. The freedom and time to be creative is a privilege and something that should not be taken for granted.

We are reminded of birthdays every year. But no one welcomes what might be interpreted as a snide comment about aging printed on "happy" birthday card. When our physical bodies age in different unique ways, general commiseration seems inappropriate. The mood has shifted and continued on a trajectory such that we now, instead of saying, "Sympathize with me on my birthday," as our mother's generation would have done, say, "Celebrate with me; celebrate who I am, today, now."

This is our time; we have earned it. Our mothers laid down the paving stones for us to walk on but we do not need to stay on the path—we owe it to ourselves and each other to explore and navigate new passages. We should use this time, without apology, and without guilt, because how we live today will reflect on the generations of women who will follow us.

Deidre

"I don't want to enter my seventies as frumpy, lumpy, and grumpy. That was the angry version of me who started the decade of my sixties. I've allowed my emotions to rule most of my life and accepted the consequences, without question, as being part of me. *It's just who I am,* I tell myself. It's as if there are twins inside me, with one twin that encourages me to do things that I know are bad for me and avoid things that are good for me, and this twin is more powerful than the other, more rational twin who's overwhelmed by her emotional sibling.

I don't have to be that way anymore. I don't need to be ruled by my emotions; it's a choice. That was very difficult for me to understand and accept, and this decade, the decade of my seventies, could be my last chance to deal with my emotions and be the best version of me. Finally. For me."

Martha

"There are days when I feel as if the journey to my seventies has been an express train ride and that I should've taken more time to savor each decade on the trip. I know that sounds like regret, and it's too late to do anything about it now. If I want to, I can rewrite all my memories, as my memory seems flexible and is definitely selective, according to my spouse, so I'm free to create whatever version I want in my own mind, my version of events of the past. But I think it's better to accept slowing down and to hop on a passenger train that stops at every station and savor the experience of the journey."

Caroline

"It took an entire decade, my sixties, to settle into a new me, and by the time I'd identified her and learned to live with her, I was about to turn seventy."

Meg

"When I look at myself, I see a picture of a woman who is comfortable, happy to be in her sixties, and ready to be in her seventies. I've come to terms with my life so far, and I'm here to enjoy the rest of it."

Chapter Twenty-Four

Anna

Something for me

Many things changed for Anna in her sixties—more changes than in previous decades— and although she adapted to the changes, she still feared not knowing the person she would be in her seventies, an unknown version of herself.

"I'm really fearful about turning seventy. It just seems as if it's all over. While I know that there are many vibrant, active women in their seventies, and even their eighties, I'm trying to figure out my version of being vibrant. I am active. Sometimes I think I've come to terms with the number, mostly by telling myself daily, *You're going to be seventy soon,* but this is followed by a second thought: *and what are you going to do about it?*'

I force myself not to groan or feel self-pity as I approach my birthday, but I am stuck in the idea that seventy signals the beginning of the end and while the 'beginning' of my life was long ago, I'm not ready to give up the 'middle' yet, let alone start the 'end.'

My sixties have been so-so, with some really high points particularly with family and friends, and some low points and disappointments with unexpected health issues and the deterioration of a relationship that I once had great hopes for. I've been divorced for eight years and I have two children who are grown and live in different states with their spouses. Each child has a grandchild on the way and, once the babies are born, I expect to see them several times a year. I like living in this town, where the children were born and raised, and I'm reluctant to give up my house and downsize, as I enjoy having my friends over and entertaining. I was in a relationship after my divorce and thought the connection might lead to something long-term but I wasn't ready to embark on what would have been a new and different way to live my life with someone else.

The most useful, if sometimes painful, part of being in my sixties was coming to terms with my life so far, really facing the realities of missed opportunities as well as successes that if I am honest, no one cares about. It's not as if there's a scoreboard that you can add your accomplishments to so everyone can see them. Getting divorced was a disappointing part of my sixties. Even though we both realized that the relationship had run its course, I, for one, did not want the upheaval and changes to my life when he left, and when I feel alone, I miss my ex. I recognize that the loss I feel is about the life we had in the past, not the life we had recently, the life we were living before we parted from each other.

I retired last year. But as I said, no one cares about what I did, what I used to do, who I used to be. Every day, that part of my life feels further and further away, in the rearview mirror. The things you accomplish in a career are all building blocks for the next step along, and when there are no next steps, the accomplishments are invalid. Learning not to care about things that I once prioritized, learning to let go, was a big lesson, and I am sometimes dumbfounded by the fact that it took me this long.

In the process of self-reflection, I realized that the changes in my routine were contributing to my confusion. My parents couldn't wait to retire, and retirement for them meant moving more slowly, clinging to a routine, and eventually down-sizing and moving several hundred miles away where their world seemed smaller than ever. They complained about a lack of friends and that no one came to see them.

Once I retired, instead of my calendar being filled with meetings and appointments, it was mostly blank, except for doctor, dentist, and hair appointments. I felt as if I'd become a cliche, an older woman looking to fill her days while she marked time. 'Let me check my calendar,' I say to people, but I don't know why, as the calendar is mostly blank.

Generally, I have a positive outlook and it was clear that I needed a new approach. I started with, '*Who do I want to be in my seventies?*' Instead of moaning about being seventy, I should see it as an opportunity to do as much as possible in the next decade as the eighties are less certain. Heeding the wisdom of others to stay connected to people, I began volunteering—something I had not done much of in my life—and although I viewed it as a cliche and the domain of retired people, I did meet other people. While I didn't like everyone I met, if I'm honest—age makes you choosy and I wish I was less judgmental— being around people was often better than being alone in my house.

All my life I've wanted to be able to draw, to put what I see in my mind's eye on paper but I've never been any good. I have a closet full of papers of different weights and beautiful crayons and markers and pencils. My favorite stores are paper supply and stationery stores. I took an online class and learned some things but it wasn't satisfying enough. I just didn't rate myself highly, and although there was no pass/fail, I just didn't connect with what was being taught.

What I failed to understand at the time was that I could just draw just for me; my drawings didn't need to have a goal. I didn't need to start a business, build a website, sell my work, or rate my success. And because I didn't want to give my friends my artwork—everyone needs less stuff as they age, not more stuff—I just pinned up all the drawings in the guest bathroom. I'm sorry to say that my children will have to figure out what to do with all my drawings one day, when I'm gone. If they rip them off the wall and put everything in the trash, I won't know anything about it.

I draw every day; it's become a habit, something I look forward to upon waking up, and I have even ventured outside to draw. Some of my efforts even make me laugh—and learning to laugh at myself has also been enjoyable—as the drawings seem so, well, inadequate, but then I'm just judging myself. Curiously enough, allowing myself the freedom to explore something that's long been concealed inside me has given me courage to try other things, and I'm getting past the point of thinking everything I try out as being an expected behavior of a retired person. Drawing gives me a warm feeling, as if I'm finally doing something for me that is not expected of me.

As seventy is around the corner, I am starting to see that what I make of being in my seventies is up to me. Aging is inevitable, but how I age and what I fill my time with, and my attitude, well, that's all on me."

Mary

"To avoid experiencing the emotional changes I was going through in my sixties, I tried to intellectualize them. In rationalizing the past, I was avoiding feeling anxious or frightened about what would happen as I reached seventy. But suppressing my feelings didn't work. I looked older and my body reflected my age, and after a while, I realized that I would have to come to terms with myself, to self-reflect, and figure out a way forward. It was a hard exercise, but a necessary one, and now I feel much happier and more content with myself as I enter the last few years of my sixties."

Chapter Twenty-Five

Valerie Newman

Reaching for dreams

A two-time breast cancer survivor, Valerie reoriented her life after divorcing her husband just before her seventieth birthday. Her view is that the experience of life asks tremendous courage of each of us, but that life's bounties are endless. She has just downsized her goal from living to ninety-five to living to ninety.

"I had a spectacular decade in my sixties, a decade of fun and joy. I will be seventy-four in 2025. Every day I feel grateful to be on this planet. I've downsized my goal to live to ninety (from ninety-five) as most people die before ninety and I want to have peers during my final years. Ninety is ambitious. I have a great run ahead of me, during which I'll continue to cut myself some slack—a lifetime problem.

Although I've always been an optimist, I've had a few major challenges. I am a breast cancer survivor (twice at the ages of fifty-eight and sixty-five). The first diagnosis came when my daughter (now thirty-three years old) was grad-uating from college. I was standing on a razor's edge while not knowing what the outcome would be. My biggest fear was that I would leave her before she was ready. But my attitude is that we face whatever obstacle is presented to us and absorb it into our ongoing lives as best as we can. During that time, when I had a mastectomy, radiation, and reconstruction, my wonderful lifetime friends were essential. It's been fifteen years since the original diagnosis, and I barely remember the first year.

Most of what I remember of the first bout with breast cancer has to do with supporting my daughter in her tran-sition to adulthood post-college, watching her in a new job where she thrived, witnessing the beginning of, and the end of, her first real relationship, and experiencing her living away from home. She was making her own life and I was meeting her where she was, as an adult woman. I wasn't always successful in that endeavor, but I kept try-ing. Separation between an adult and an only child is a unique challenge.

Between the two diagnoses, I've made the most of my life. I've had fun, a lot of fun. I've learned a lot—mostly to listen to my own voice and take full responsibility for the rest of my life. Just shy of my seventieth birthday, I divorced my husband, and we went our separate ways. This was the right decision, but a very tough decision. There's a price to pay for any major life event and I found that the first year after the divorce was the hardest. My head would spin during the 'firsts' of all traditional holiday events, such as birthdays, holidays, and anniversaries. 'This too shall pass' is a favorite motto of mine. In time, the spinning subsided.

During my sixties, I traveled extensively around the country with my spouse. A ninety-day motorhome trip from Seattle to Los Angeles and Florida (and back) was inspiring and restful. I loved the breadth and size of our country, the range of topography, the small and medium towns, and the major cities along the way, and the distinct cultures in all regions. And I loved the freedom to hike, golf, needlepoint, and read along the way. I met nice people everywhere. Learning about US history through travel was enthralling and informative.

I've been fortunate enough to travel abroad as well, and the experiences mirrored those of my domestic adventures. Most people are great; they share themselves, look after each other, and take immense pride in their communities. We're more alike, globally, than we may think. I found language and cultural differences inspiring, uplifting, and motivating—in short, full of hope.

Now I've nearly completed the first five years of my seventies. My friends ask, 'Can you believe we're seventy-four and still feel forty-five?' While I have great energy, enthusiasm, and curiosity, this positivity is dampened by things that can depress me. I'm slowing down, physically, and mentally, and losing family and friends. I often find myself asking myself, *What did I come into this room for?* Fearful of tripping up or down stairs, I focus on counting the stairs one at a time, never multitasking, and I always have one hand on the banister. I feel a narrowing of my world, which will continue through my eighties, but I'm not afraid.

I loved studying French in college, and in 2025 I took a four-week-long French language immersion course in France. Eight hours a day, from nine a.m. until five p.m., speaking only French. There were downsides such as being one of the oldest of twenty-five students; most were in their forties to sixties. I am now slower to learn, but I persisted and graduated and I loved it. I believe that reaching your dreams is doable. I want to be the person who dreams and reaches for as long as I live.

Living without fear is a choice, a difficult choice, but it is my choice. I remind myself every single day, when confronting small or massive things that it's possible to accomplish a great deal if you face challenges head-on, with minor adjustments for lesser physical and mental capabilities. I appreciate nature more, read even more books, and take long vigorous walks. My family is important to me, and I have long talks with my brother and sister who live locally. We lost our younger brother in 2012 and his absence changed my world, as I was his first big sister and looked out for him from my earliest memories. The pain remains. I believe that I'll be with him again.

I'm thriving today but admit that meeting new friends in a new community at this age is challenging. It's hard to find people with like-minded values and interests. As a long-time volunteer, I've found solid relationships and volunteering provides a feeling of well-being. I also play golf with a wonderful group of women. At seventy-four, I remind myself to appreciate differences, to listen, and to stay in my own lane.

Life may not be fair, but it is a wonder."

Valerie Newman, Washington State, USA

Kim

"To be honest, I entered the decade of my sixties without having given much thought to the idea of legacy, about what I would leave behind and how I would be remembered. I don't think many women think about this. But after a health issue in my mid-sixties, I began to think hard about what I had accomplished and what I still wanted to accomplish before I turned seventy. Seventy. How would I be remembered by my family and friends? Life is full of choices—perhaps we are spoiled for choice? The most important thing was to take the time to think about this, seriously, think about this. I don't want to just drift into my seventies and then beyond. I still have time to work out the shape of my life in the next decade."

Epilogue - Last words

If you are sixty-two, or even sixty-four, and reading this book you may wonder why the concept of legacy is relevant to women in their sixties. For you, it may be too soon to start thinking about much to do with aging at all. But your sixties will spin by fast, and there will come a point when the idea of legacy is one that comes to mind frequently.

In 2021 I decided that, if I was lucky and took good care of myself, I would live to be in my early to mid-eighties. That works for me. I do not want to be a burden on anyone, dependent on anyone, needing support and robbing others of their time and resources. I've seen this happen too often, families having to compromise to take care of an elderly relative, often with love, blended with an unwelcome—and unspoken—dose of resentment. Accommodations have to be altered, finances adjusted, and going away on a trip might mean finding someone to look after an elderly relative as well as walk and feed the family dog. There comes a time for all of us to move along.

I like my life and feel fortunate in being able to say that. It is a privilege. I love the people in my life. Would I live it differently—? Some of it, looking back, of course, I would have made different decisions, but I have come to terms with my life, and myself. When people ask, "What would you say to your younger self?" my response is this: first of all, I'm not sure that I would recognize my younger self, and secondly, I am certain that she would never have listened to any of my advice.

So, if things go according to plan, that means approximately fifteen or sixteen more summers, fifteen or sixteen more winters, fifteen or sixteen more birthday celebrations. When you frame your life this way, you'll want to account for the past and enjoy every minute of the present and the future. Who has time to be bored?

So, here I am: *Georgina O'Hara Callan 1956* —

We don't know the date; no one knows the date, the time, the place or the circumstances. When you write it out like this, it becomes real, the thing most of us do not want to think about; that is, the concept of our mortality.

I know that I don't want to take a passive approach, sitting quietly in the corner waiting for the appointed moment, and perhaps you feel the same way. Armed with the insights of the decade of our sixties, we can use our remaining time well and reach out and up for a way to live our life with an idea, a sense, of our legacy— how we want to be remembered, by the people who are important to us, and by the people we love and who love us. They see us, but we cannot look through their eyes and see ourselves.

In our sixties, we get to shape the rest of our lives, and in the process, we can become a new generation of older women, defined not by earlier ideas of women in their sixties, seventies, and eighties, but by new versions of self, one woman at a time.

Essayists A - Z

Carol Ascher, Social Justice Advocate, New Orleans, Louisiana, USA. https://www.sonofasaint.org

Professor Barbara Bernier, Educational/Legal Consultant, Florida, USA. "Federal Inquiry of Charlotte Law School Is Disclosed by Suit". (*New York Times*, September 13, 2017). https://barbarabernier.com

Lori J Bridges-Hahn, Author, Ohio, USA. "Letters to Eric," "Wilhelmina."

M.J. Buckman, (Em Buckman), Author, UK. "Bent Is Not Broken," "Women of Note." https://mjbuckman.com

Peggy Gerber, Author, New Jersey, USA. "Stumbling in Crazy Town," "The Big Indignity," "Once Upon a Time Machine."

Eileen Keller, Social Physicist and Media Investment Strategist, Austin, Texas, USA. https://www.ideality.com

Elise Krentzel, Ghost Writer, Book Coach, Author, Austin, Texas, USA. https://elisekrentzel.com

Deborah Main Jones Latimer, Entrepreneur, Austin, Texas, USA. https://www.thepillowgoddess.com

Leslie McKenna, Writer, Bedfordshire, UK. Tales From the House of Words and Memory.

Lena Samson, Board of Directors Member, Ottawa Independent Writers, Ottawa, Canada. https://ottowaindependentwriters.com

Silvia Smith, Author, Ontario, Canada. "Figs Beneath the Snow," "This Strange New Path: Poetry to Heal from Narcissistic Abuse."

Acknowledgments

I am sincerely grateful to all the women who have contributed to this book in one way or another, from the essayists who penned their heartfelt words, to the women who shared conversations with me that enabled me to help write—and share—their stories. I would also like to thank the readers who provided feedback on the early manuscript including Melanie Robb, Kindy Verderber, Samantha Greenfield, Judy Devlin, Nancy Craft, and thanks also goes to my editor, Claire Dunn.

About the author

G eorgina O'Hara Callan's early career began in London, UK, as a women's magazine journalist, a ghost writer, and a magazine editor. Her first book was about financial advice for women, written at a time when many women did not have full control over their own money.

For her second book, she spent a year in Paris, France, researching the history of fashion and fashion design from the early 1800s, when the invention of the home sewing machine became a functional and creative tool for many women, simultaneously changing fashion forever. Research for the book required extensive travel to the USA and within the UK and Europe. *The Thames & Hudson Dictionary of Fashion and Fashion Designers* was translated into multiple languages, and *Vogue* labeled the book a "fashion bible."

After moving to the USA in 1985, Georgina published two more books, one on infancy and the culture of nurture over the centuries, and the other on the social history of marriage and how the original business and contractual arrangement of marriage has changed over the centuries.

Georgina lived for twenty years in New Orleans, Louisiana, and after Hurricane Katrina (in 2005), moved to Dallas, Texas where she continued to raise her sons, who are now grown with families of their own.

After several decades, when she paused writing to raise a family and start a design and textiles business, causing her to travel extensively nationally and internationally, Georgina returned to writing, at first by interviewing architects, designers, and creatives for various publications. She describes her life as being "book-ended." She started writing in her twenties and now in her sixties—after a life full of experiences and many tales to tell— she is writing once again. *Sixty and Speaking Up* is her fifth book.